CREDIT SCORE

The Complete Guide to Improve Your Credit Score
Including Letter Templates to Take Action

(Quick and Easy Way to Repair Your Credit and
Increase Your Credit Score)

Steven Solis

Published By Bella Frost

Steven Solis

All Rights Reserved

Credit Score: The Complete Guide to Improve Your Credit Score Including Letter Templates to Take Action (Quick and Easy Way to Repair Your Credit and Increase Your Credit Score)

ISBN 978-1-77485-361-0

Legal & Disclaimer

The information contained in this book is not designed to replace or take the place of any form of medicine or professional medical advice. The information in this book has been provided for educational and entertainment purposes only.

The information contained in this book has been compiled from sources deemed reliable, and it is accurate to the best of the Author's knowledge; however, the Author cannot guarantee its accuracy and validity and cannot be held liable for any errors or omissions. Changes are periodically made to this book. You must consult your doctor or get professional medical advice before using any of the suggested remedies, techniques, or information in this book.

TABLE OF CONTENTS

Introduction

Being rich is a goal that is commonplace, but, only a handful of people manage to achieve it. In the present day when credit cards are the norm it is impossible for anyone to save and still have that small amount of money in their account when they finish each month. Shopping for food, clothes and other items can lead to spending several hundred dollars.

Add in the numerous fees for mortgages and loans to pay , and they are left with a small amount of money. This kind of scenario is common in businesses that have to borrow large amounts of money from lenders to ensure that the company is able to continue to operate.

These kinds of situations can cause an individual or a company to have bad credit, which can cause them nightmares. If you're one of the company or person who is in the bad times and isn't sure what to do to fix the issue and fix it, then you've found the right website.

In this Book I will provide to you everything you should be aware of about credit scores and how to fix your score with a minimum of effort. I will also discuss the mistakes you should not do if you have a low credit score so that you aren't making these errors.

Let's begin.

Chapter 1: Dispute the Charges

It is important to monitor your credit score. There are a lot of credit card companies and websites that offer this service for absolutely free, so be sure that you're benefiting from this option. You'll be able monitor any time someone steals your identity, and you're being able to monitor the accounts that affect your credit score, both positive and negative.

If you check the credit reports and find lots of negative credit accounts, including collections or accounts that are past due take a look at whether they're true. Do you realize that companies that report on your credit are legally required to make sure you have a credit report that is correct at all times? If it's not , they're legally required (also under the law) to erase the inaccurate information.

What this means for you is that should the negative reports in your credit file aren't completely accurate, you can request that they be taken off. What you need to do is examine your credit report to determine which ones could not be true. Keep in mind that you're not permitted to challenge the truth of anything. Therefore, if the negative report that appears on your credit reports is true, you're required to let it be. If not, send an email to the credit reporting company (that's Transunion, Equifax or Experian) and request for them to take it off. Tell them the reason why it should be taken off and ensure that you include your birthdate, name and your social security number on the letter.

If you do this , you must notify the agency that reports on credit. has to examine and verify the account is in fact accurate. If it's not, they will issue an acknowledgement letter and request that if they have proof that the account isn't correct, you provide your data to them. If it's not correct, they will remove it from your credit report. Your credit rating will then be revised to reflect the change.

Sending letters to credit bureaus doesn't always yield 100% results. Sometimes, they'll claim that an account is verified even though you are aware that it's not accurate. If this happens, you'll need to step over their heads and send a letter to the creditor who originally issued the account informing them that the account isn't accurate and providing proof of the claim. It could be a statement that shows that your charges were paid in time or letters that state that they've closed the account. Make sure you send the copies but not the original letter.

Incorrect information can result in many accounts closed and could also help you get rid of certain debts as you will not be required to pay debt collection or past due charges if you demonstrate that they aren't correct. In addition, it will boost your credit score and improve your credit score as the bad accounts are getting wiped out.

Chapter 2: It's (Mostly) Everything

About the Payments

"The person who has no enough money to cover his debts is in need of other things."
James Lendall Basford

The most important factor in determining how your score is assessed, no matter the agency that generates credit has, it's your capacity to make your payments as they become due. If you're looking to boost your credit score and maintain it there it is essential to do everything you can to ensure that you pay your bills on time or sooner if it is possible. Here are some ways you can make payments to improve the credit rating of your.

Fast and prompt payment

Because your credit history makes up the largest part in your score late or missed payments account for 35 percent in your score immediately! This is so simple to remember until it becomes disadvantageous.

What's the problem? It's so simple to overlook it and end up with the payment being late or not made. It's like the person whom you never think about since they're always there i.e. they're easy to reach. It's the reason why although it's common sense to not miss payments or pay late it's important to be reminded of this.

Today's technology to ensure that late or missed payments to the financial obligation you have is almost impossible. The first step is to sign up for an automatic payments arrangement with your bank. this option is the easiest, and is worth the time to implement. Since it's automated, the capability to deprive you of the chance to pay your debts on time will be eliminated completely. This is, however, assuming that your accounts are in good condition of course. But what happens if there's not enough funds to cover your obligations regularly?

One of the most effective ways to go about it is contact the institution that you are owed money. Find out if they are possible to alter the due date to a date later that will give you plenty of time and space for a timely payment.

What happens if your monthly budget is the same than your leggings following eating a buffet meal on a day when you had a fast? That's a completely different tale right there. If you're in credit to be considered a good candidate, why not attempt to combine or consolidate all the debt you have into one loan with a lower interest rate. If this isn't an option try talking to your creditors and asking for an extended grace period or reduced interest. It's not a bad idea to try. If you are successful then you might be able to reduce how much of your financial obligations to the point that you are able to begin paying each month on time.

The last option, if the lower interest rate doesn't work for you, is to bargain with your creditors about the restructuring of your current obligations. When I say restructuring, I'm referring to increasing the amount of time or years you have to pay the debts you owe, without being slapped with high interest , penalties or fees. It might seem like a long-shot, but it's not a bad idea to try and failing could turn out to be financially disastrous for you.

If you're able to access funds, you should make sure that timely payments on time. It doesn't matter if you want your bank's help to remember or stick to a traditional calendars made of paper.

Increase the Frequency of Your Payment

One of the most costly mistakes you can make regarding your payments and your score on credit is to assume that you're fine when you meet your debts - especially your credit cards , because they're due each month, regardless of whether you're prone to over-limit your credit limits or are always close to exceeding them. What's the reason for this? The reason is that the banks which you borrowed funds from only make it clear that your balances are outstanding once each month. This can result in large reported monthly balances which could cause credit scoring agencies to think that you're not using enough credit facility. In turn, this increases your perceived credit risk, which in turn could result in less credit score.

It could sound complicated , so ponder for a minute and allow me to show an example. Let's say that your credit card is able to hold $1,500 . Even better is that it gives you rewards. This is why you're likely to make use of it as frequently that you are able to, almost the limit every month to earn reward. When the bill is due, you can pay it in full. For the non-expert financial mind it's an excellent method to make use of credit cards. However, for those who know something concerning credit scores and especially the ratio of credit to debt, this is certainly not something to make cartwheels about.

Based on the scenario above it would appear to the credit scoring agency that you're always over or close to exceeding your credit limit. Since they take only the numbers into account and do not have the time or resources to inquire about why you're using almost the entire allowance, they'll simply take the figures at face value and suppose that your risk to credit is very high because of problems with your finances or inability manage your spending. It's obvious how this could affect the score of your credit, don't you? Right?

The best solution could be making smaller, but more frequent monthly payments. For instance, you could pay off your balance each week, so it appears that your balances on the books are less which is beneficial to your score on credit. Instead of paying it all in one go when your bill is due, you can pay off everything each week or every two weeks. If you do this you'll be able to have your cake of rewards and eat it as well!

Balances Past Due

When you default on a payment the account will eventually be viewed as being overdue. When your account gets increasingly late the creditors may resort to more severe or even extreme measures to make sure that your account is updated with regards to payments.

If your accounts are only a little overdue and your creditors' efforts to collect may not be that significant, i.e., you might only receive a pleasant reminder by phone or text message to remind you that you have did not pay your bill and that you need to get it done as soon as you are able. If your account is increasingly late, i.e., the amount of time it's overdue and the more serious actions that your creditors might take, such as warnings of legal actions such as bankruptcy or legal cases. In terms of credit scores, the more time your account is due the lower your component score - and therefore your overall credit score will be.

If you've got outstanding account, here are a few options to rectify this issue, which can improve your credit score and help get it back in good shape. One option is to pay the entire amount in one drop. This way you will be able to restore your credit score to the realm of the living and , in the process to bring your credit score back to the glory of its former self. But the greater the sum of your overdue balance is the higher the minimum payment will be because interest and costs would have already been added to the total amount. It's the most effective and fastest method to ensure that your account isn't completely dying or being transferred to mortuary or collection agencies, and taking your credit score with it .

Another method to deal with the past due balances to get the credit rating back to normal is to get caught up on your payments. In reality, paying off the whole outstanding balance could be too challenging to complete by making a single lump amount payment. Make contact with your creditors and ask them to negotiate that you are allowed to settle your outstanding balances in 3 to six months, if required. In this means you'll be able to gradually eliminate your balances due.

If your creditors do not formally accept a staggered payment of balances that are past due? Add additional payment until the time you're ready complete the catch-up and restore your account's status to current. Keep in mind that even if you're making the catch up payments, they'll be considered to be past due. The account will be reinstated back to the "current" status when you've made all your catch-up payment, i.e., settle the balances that are due in total. If you're not able to make the necessary payments before the date your account that is due to be paid becomes at least 180 days old, the account might be fully charged by your creditors, and could damage your credit and payment history. score.

Re-Age Your past due account

If you're able to pay the entire amount of the outstanding balance, without having to pay interest or charges that add up in a way that isn't appropriate, it would be beneficial to inquire with your lender if it's possible to reset or re-age your account due. Why? Doing so can make your delinquencies vanish. Although creditors aren't required to re-age their accounts due to past due Some do consent to Re-age these accounts, especially when it's the first time that they've become past due. There's no harm asking and why shouldn't you?

Consolidation of Debt

When you consolidate debts, particularly the past instalments, they won't receive the chance to pay them entirely. What it does , however, is to bring them up which makes them easier to settle and extremely unlikely to be charged and all of these are major positives for the credit rating of yours.

Consolidating your debts is to take care of those that are old and create another. This is the reason I mentioned that the consolidation won't assist in the payment of the debts you owe in one go. Since you'll be taking on new debts it is essential that prior to you agree to the consolidation you've read the terms and conditions in detail and thoroughly. By doing this, you can avoid getting a shock by subsequent increases in interest rates and amount of payments when the honeymoon period comes to an end.

Speak and negotiate

If everything else fails and you believe it's impossible for you to make changes to your payment schedule, then you may attempt to negotiate a potential settlement for your debtors. This settlement option could be one where the creditor accepts an amount that is smaller than the lump sum payment required to end the obligation. It is usually a matter of negotiations to cancel the exorbitant charges and interest in order to lower the total amount due and permit the total payment of the exact outstanding amount. A cautionary note to this approach is that you should ensure that when you reach out to your creditors to negotiate the smaller lump-sum amount you have the funds to make your lump-sum payment. Many creditors are willing to accept this kind of settlement since they know that at the end of day they'll be content to receive their money back along with a reasonable interest rate because they are aware that, in many instances insisting on the amount they believe is due to them can lead to eventually writing off debt. Therefore, you should never believe that you can have such good faith when you're looking to resolve your accounts that are past due and breathe new life into your credit rating.

Use Your Card To Pay Rent, Utilities, Etc.

In terms of your payment history, it's not only the amount of your debt that is important. Credit scoring companies or agencies take a look at your achievements in making payments, i.e., the payments you were able to pay in time. It's no surprise that the more regular payments you make regularly and the better you are able to demonstrate your ability to meet your debts when they become over due i.e. lower credit risk. Since you credit score based on assessing your credit risk that means more successful payments translate into an improved credit score.

So, if you're looking to boost your credit score and improve your credit history, utilize your card more often by paying regularly-recurring costs that you're usually in a position to pay promptly with cash, for example, utility bills and rent. Make sure to pay them off every couple of weeks as we mentioned in the previous chapter - to improve the credit rating of your. Make sure that you don't "max out" often with your credit limits. You should also keep your ratio of credit utilization to a reasonable level that we'll cover in greater detail in the following chapter.

Chapter 3: Store Charge Cards

Another option to build your credit score is to request a charge card in a department store near you. Credit from department stores is typically more accessible in comparison to credit cards from banks.

Many vendors and retailers offer credit to customers with weak or no credit history. If you own a major credit card like Visa or MasterCard, getting a Department Store credit card is easy.

Simply present your main credit card, along with a photograph identification or driver's licence, fill out a credit application, and you're granted credit.

Don't apply for multiple credit cards at the same time. All inquiries will be added to your credit report every time you make an application for credit. Multiple inquiries can be detrimental to your credit rating and may result in you being denied.

Sign up to become an authorized user

This is the process of convincing your friend or family member to add them to the existing credit card. This is a widely recommended and a convenient method to add positive details to your credit account.

You'll be added to the credit card account of the individual. This means that you will benefit from another person's excellent repayment record. The card that has your name is sent directly to the cardholder who is primary. When the card is activated, you'll have the same purchasing ability that the cardholder who is primary.

Ask your friend or family member to make contact with the credit card company to confirm that they record the account on your credit report.

Find A Cosigner

If you aren't able to qualify on account of your credit rating, think about having co-signers. A co-signer could be a family member or friend or another person who will accept to pay back your debt should you default.

Find someone with a strong credit history to cosign the application for credit or loan. In cosigning on behalf of you they are legally binding to make the loan payment if you do not.

As a cosigner guarantees to pay you if you don't make the payments required and this will greatly increase the chances of getting credit.

If you do not pay your debts you could ruin the credit score of the co-signer.

Any new credit you receive make sure you use it wisely. The best rule of thumb is to never spend more than half of your credit limit.

Maintaining a Good Credit Rating

1. You should try to get credit from those who are reported the credit bureaus. This will build your credit score. When you are applying for credit, you should find out whether the creditor will report credit credit bureaus in your region.

2. Make sure you pay your bills in time starting today. If you're unable to concentrate or simply overwhelmed, consider automating your payment. It is

possible to set up automatic payments with your creditor's automatic payment system or the bill-paying service of your bank online. You must ensure that you have enough funds in your account at the bank to pay for the cost of these automated payments.

3. Do not overburden yourself with obligations like installment payments or credit card debt.

4. Be careful not to exceed your limit, and pay all balances in full, or pay at least the minimum amount due every month or each billing period.

5. It is recommended that you get in touch with your creditors or lenders immediately if you experience financial problems to receive assistance to keep up to date with your accounts. Contact, write or email your creditors to inform them of how you are coping financially. If you've been punctual in paying your debts previously, your creditors could be willing to collaborate with you.

6. Credit bureaus keep track of each inquiry regarding you. A report stays on

your file for a period of two years. A lot of inquiries can make credit providers reluctant to accept a credit request. They could decline credit if they believe that you're opening more than one new account in a short period of time. Spread your requests out to give your previous inquiries the chance to be canceled in time.

7. Avoid such drastic actions as repossession, litigation or turning your account in to debt collection agency. If you're financially stressed You should consider ways to increase your income.

8. Be aware of the details on your credit report. A credit score that is good can be the key to opening many possibilities for you.

Chapter 4: The Way to Refuse Bad Credit Even If It is You Own Bad Credit

The first thing to consider is that you may actually be inclined to hire an attorney, or even a financial specialist to fix your poor credit. However, this isn't always the best option. While it might seem like great to turn your credit score in the shortest amount of period of time, but it might not be the right choice that you have.

The cost of starting may be excessive and you are able to easily alter your credit yourself. Credit scores aren't changed over night; they can be a long time, but perhaps not for years however, a bit of time to see improvement. There are some companies that claim they can turn the credit score within one day, but that will not occur.

It requires an enormous amount of effort to repair bad credit. There will come a times when you have to contest the negative credit you have on your credit report. While businesses can help however, it's best to handle this on your own. Working with a third party can be confusing, and negotiating with creditors directly is much more enjoyable.

So , how do you fight negative credit in your credit score?

The first step is to have to take a look the credit reports. Actually, you may get an absolutely complimentary credit score. There are a variety of ways to get a free credit history report. So don't be afraid to request yours!

You can request a free report by contacting Trans Union, Equifax or Experian after you have received your report, it is recommended to go through it completely.

This is a matter of checking it thoroughly and attentively, and sometimes it is necessary to go over the report with a fine toothcomb twenty times. If you happen to find something in the report that you don't like it is possible to make a note of the report.

But, before you start charging like an ox in the china shop, make sure to verify whether the negative report was deleted from your credit report by when you checked the report, and then a few weeks afterward. The majority of credit bureaus update the data they collect often , so they will remove it within several weeks.

File a Dispute Online

If you are looking to dispute an inaccurate credit report, you can do it online. You'll have to file a complaint on the internet at the website of a credit bureau. You'll have to submit a form to the website , and you will need to specify the negative report or reports you wish to challenge. Also, you must provide the reasons for why you would like to contest it.

After you've completed this you can make a copy of it to keep for your own documents. The amount of time it takes for a credit bureau to reply can differ. It could be as long as 24 hours or even weeks, therefore be patient.

If you discover that 30 or a month days have gone by and there are no signs of contact by the credit bureau you can call to inquire about what's happening. Most of the time you'll hear back from them.

It could take up to 30 days be patient and wait until that period has ended since the bureau must examine the issue. If they are in agreement with you they must rectify the issue also, which requires time. If you've succeeded, however, you will be issued a your credit report updated.

If you're not satisfied with the outcome, contact and ask the creditor to clarify the negative report. Keep in mind that the credit bureaus are only able to be guided by the information provided by the creditor's data, therefore, don't blame them when the decision doesn't work out your way. There could be an error on the part of the creditor.

If there has been poor credit from your side You can request the creditor to could take it off. This can help your credit score in the end.

However, even if would like to challenge bad credit even if it's yours

Can You Disputate Anything Even if it's Correct?

Anybody can challenge everything on their credit reports. We should not get involved in the morality debate since some people contest everything, while others will contest nothing. It is entirely up to each person's personal decision.

You are entitled to have each and every bit of information in your credit report 100% exact. You'll want verified details on your credit report as well! Also, you may contest any information that appears in the credit file.

What Can You Do To Disput a Matter Without Going online?

If you are planning to bring a case then you must draft an extremely polite, courteous but complete letter. It is important to write the letter carefully and state that you'd like a specific piece of information that is verified and, if the information can't be verified, you should remove this information from your report.

Don't claim that the correct information needs to be removed from your report.

Instead, you should say that you'd like to have something verified. A credit report will make talks with your lender and verify the information or disputed.

Are You Able to Resolve a Difference?

If you have a dispute with the credit score of someone else you are able to re-dispute the issue. The process involves completing a dispute form, and you will be asked to provide the reason for why you should dispute it once again. The results may be identical If you could contact the lender and speak to them, you may be able to settle the dispute.

Sometimes the credit bureau may not review a new dispute, so you have be aware of this.

What you need to remember

Your credit reports are crucial because they include all of the important details about you on it. They include information like your address of previous financial status, your bank accounts and even how much you spend on your credit card each month. every month! The report also includes information about whether or not you've previously filed bankruptcy, or even been sued, as plus a lot more details.

Be aware that all the information in your credit report will determine whether you're able to get an upcoming loan. It will also influence the amount you are able to take out and the way you will have to pay back the loan in addition. This is why it's crucial to keep only correct current and, of course, complete information included on it.

False information can be detrimental to you , even if it's just a year old. It could work against you when purchasing major items. If you want to buy an automobile or mortgage, the amount you can take out could be a problem and, more importantly is that if your credit score was in a bad state it could mean that you won't be able to buy the home you want!

This is why it's vital to keep your credit report current to the current.

Chapter 5: The Way to Solve Indebtedness.

While creditors would like to believe that way, the truth to the contrary is every amount you owe can be negotiated. Furthermore regardless of the size, 90% of creditors will offer an amount in one lump sum today instead of an agreement to pay it in the future. If you are trying to negotiate big sums, these guidelines can make it easier to win.

Write a story and keep it up Tell a story and stick to it: The person you're working with won't have a keen interest in the details of your the way you tell it, but they'll require to know the reason you're unable to pay the entire amount at this moment. That means that you're going need to tell an account of the hardships you have faced and describes the steps you're taking to make it work. You'll want to break your story to the essential aspects and not stray from your position throughout negotiations.

One of the most effective strategies is to mention that because of financial strain and financial hardship, you'll soon meet with lawyers who specialize in bankruptcy. This is almost always going to cause creditors to be more inclined to make a deal because when you file for bankruptcy, there is a good chance they will not receive anything.

Keep calm: It's crucial to remember that regardless of what the creditor claims, you are in the advantage since the debt you carry gives you leverage over them. Keep this in mind and, regardless of the words they use try to keep your cool. If you create a scene or cause a drama, the creditor will realize they're getting you and may not be inclined to offer a bargain. If you're feeling you're losing your cool, say that you'll contact them again and end the conversation as fast as you can. In the event that you are finding behavior of the creditor difficult to accept, simply say that you're recording the conversation, which will ensure they are on top of their game and most professional behaviour.

Always be prepared to ask questions: If a creditor threatens you with a lawsuit or losing property then it is essential to not let these threats scare your into taking a wrong choice. Instead, it's important to inquire as it can reveal whether the creditor is lying or not. For instance, if the creditor threatens you with lawsuit, you can ask when you are likely to hear about it. Note down these threats because they are usually sometimes illegal since creditors are restricted as to how they deal with the debt issue, with a particular focus on protecting consumers.

Additionally, you're likely need to record notes whenever you meet with an individual creditor, including names of those who you spoke with along with the date, time and items discussed, particularly threats. There's usually a time limit in regards to the time the creditor must collect the debt, which is different depending on the location, and are likely to become more irate as the deadline approaches.

Do not sign the payment arrangement: If you sign up to a payment schedule, you are always going to pay more over the long term even if you manage to come up with an all-in lump sum payment. Based on the amount you owe, as little as 30 percent may suffice to satisfy the lender if that it's getting close to the expiration date they will have to collect the debt. You have kept to your tale of bankruptcy and financial hardship.

Don't be afraid to give an unfavorable price and the worst thing that can occur is for them to refuse to accept the offer. If you do agree to a payment schedule, make sure to review the cost with a fine comb. Also, make sure you can pay the bill each month, so that you don't find yourself in the same spot.

Do your best to negotiate to creditors. If you're aware you'll be in a position to not pay on a debt you've amassed, try your best to negotiate an agreement directly with the creditor prior to having the debt transferred to collections. The creditor will always be to be more negotiating with than an outside debt collection company.

Maintaining credit.

After you've completed the job of repairing your credit score, you'll need to make every effort to ensure that you don't end up returning to the same place you were. You've put in the effort to rectify the mistakes that you made in the past, but don't let it as a reason to make new ones. To help you stay on the right path take a look at the following suggestions.

Make sure to pay all of your charges on time. every one of them. Although it is unlikely that every bill you have to pay will be showing up on your credit reports if you're just a few days behind when it comes time to pay it, it is impossible to be certain of what bills are crucial and which ones can be left unanswered until the next check. A minor penalty from the local library could end up ending in your credit reports, damaging your hard-earned credit score and affecting your credit score. Do not take a chance and remain attentive when it comes to making sure you pay your bills in time.

Avoid using credit cards Although credit cards can improve your credit utilization and your credit history however, using them frequently is a sure way to begin sliding backwards, particularly in the case of budgets that are at a low point. If you have to use credit cards, you should take particular care to make sure you do not surpass a credit utilization level of 30 percent, as this is the time when your credit score can begin to suffer. Although going over the limit will only hurt your credit score by just a couple of points, if your score is close to an appropriate score it could be enough to see more expensive rates due to.

Reduce your debts: After you've redressed your financial situation The best way to stay on track is to set a goal of paying off your loans as fast as you can; remember that approximately 30% of the credit rating you have is affected on the level of credit that you have that's why it's one of the most effective ways to improve your credit score once you're getting moving towards the correct direction.

In order to have more money to pay off your debt first thing you're likely to need to do is stop living paycheck to paycheck, and establishing your own emergency savings account. An emergency fund that is well-established can allow you to survive for three months and cover all of your expenses in the event that something happens and you are forced being laid off from work. The creation of this fund will allow you the flexibility to prioritize your debts and not worry about every small issue that might come up.

Spending on monitors: About 40% of people who have problems with their credit score did so simply because they didn't keep the track of their spending from week to week and spending as much as they ought to. With the popularity internet banking there's no reason to not know exactly what your balance on your checking account is at all times of every day. Make a habit of tracking your spending habits and you'll not be surprised by your bank statement when it shows at the close each month. It doesn't mean that you shouldn't be interested in looking over the statement when it arrives However, since you don't know what kind of mistake may be made. You also don't think about when a bit of diligence can be rewarded in a huge way.

Stay on top of your credit report The fact that you're not in the middle of anything doesn't mean nothing significant is likely to appear at the bottom of your report regardless of whether it's your fault or not. Some new information from your past could be revealed on your report, or some bureaus might be negligent or forget to record the positive changes you've implemented in a timely manner. These chapters offered you the necessary tools to tackle the issues however, you'll only be in a position to put these into practice when you're aware of these issues in the first place. Don't let your effort be wasted, keep using the free credit reports you receive each year.

Chapter 6: Communicating with Bureaus and Creditors

You can negotiate your way to an affordable payment

When you've taken an inventory of the debts you owe you are able to begin negotiations for the lowest amount of payment, starting with collections accounts that are not older than two years. These are the ones that have the highest negative impact upon your credit rating. In the way that debt collection operates means that your debt is most cases sold by the company that issued your initial creditor company to an debt collection firm at a substantial discount and the company is then left with the task of recouping the full amount of your debt as it is possible.

Let's take an example. Company A is an organization that collects debts. They will purchase all of Store A's negative account with a credit card. The Store A has already credited the balance due in their books of accounts as a loss, therefore they'll offer the rights to pay the debt to company A for .05 per dollar. If you have to pay Company A A $500, then Company A will purchase the their debt at $1. Then, they have a predetermined time frame to try to recover as much of that debt as they can. Economic economies of scale enable companies that collect debt to purchase huge amounts of debt that is not worth paying low prices, and that's the way they earn their money.

If you dispute or request your debts to be formally validated by the company A, you will determine the amount it cost them to pay for their debt. This provides you with a great advantage when you negotiate a discount payment. The ability to negotiate an affordable payment will differ dependent on the specifics of your case. Whatever you do, ensure that you put by writing the amount be reportedas "Paid as agreed." This will mean that when a prospective lender checks your credit file, they will not find a bad debt, but they will be able to see your report as "Paid as agreed." The debt collectors can provide the details to credit agencies however they want So, don't accept anything other than "Paid as agreed" in negotiations and make sure you get it written before you make payments.

Additionally, do not allow an individual creditor to deduct your bank account in the event that you do not set up an account separate from your bank to pay outstanding debts. Send the payment in writing or make payment using a different method that doesn't involve the debiting of your bank account. This will protect the consumer from any unwanted charges being debited from your account. As per law, creditors must to offer multiple payment options. For instance, you can pay $200 to settle the debt of $500, however the debt collector could accidentally debit your account with $500. Some debt collectors aren't so sly, but it's always better to be safer than sorry.

As a general rule you've already demonstrated to an agent that you'll pay in full by placing your account put in collections. Do not be afraid to leave negotiations for payment when the debt collector doesn't intend to come to an agreement that is in line with your conditions. If your debt is not more that two years old I would suggest offering between 40 and 60 percent of the amount that you owed originally. Their role is to collect on debt and they make an impressive commission to collect debt. Keep in mind that this is business and regardless of how nice and pleasant the conversation is If you fail to receive what you want in the negotiations you will lose. Debt collectors aren't your friends, they are performing their duties.

Make and share your own story of financial success

Before you have your account sent to collections when you are experiencing difficult times, you should write an explanation of your circumstances in writing to the creditor. This should be done before your account is deemed 60 or 90 days over due. It is possible to request the payment to be reduced for a certain amount of time. You could request an extended period of forbearance or you could request for a month's installment to is added at the final balance of the note if it's for the installment plan. In the business world, everything is negotiable which means you can make any request you like and the lender will respond in a manner that is appropriate. Like any other kind of partnership, communication is crucial.

There are many other people who can provide information regarding your credit file. It is also possible to send an official letter to each bureau of credit with an individual statement. This could include a short summary of a financial difficulty that leads two accounts to be delinquent. In the event of a reason, you are able to include any statement on the credit file. This will help a potential lender to better understand the reason there are accounts that have been reported as to be 30 days late over the last 24 months. The consumer statement could ultimately aid you in getting favorable loan approval when you have rectified a lot of your negative account data at the time of this statement.

Alongside having your consumer statement included on your credit score, you could take a look at the relatively new self-reporting method. One website and service provider which is gaining popularity for reporting self is called the Pay Rent Build Credit. To receive an PRBC Report and Score and Report, become a member and sign up for at least three accounts that are billed monthly. This could include your rent, your electric bill, cable bill, or perhaps your online bill. All you need to do is that you pay your bills on time each month. PRBC may not have the authority of the three major credit bureaus, however an impressive report from PRBC could suffice to get your first step of the lender.

Each city has local associations that provide assistance to those seeking credit counseling. Should they not have one, it must be one within an hour drive.

Financial knowledge is becoming more commonplace as the young people continue to progress to their highest income earning years. Make sure you take advantage of the tools available to you. There is hope and a light towards the other end even if you're experiencing financial difficulties that are not satisfactory regardless of race or nationality. In the current Digital Age, you only have to make use of your freedom of imagination to discover many opportunities for you along with your entire family.

In the same way, according to the data by the numbers, millennials (people born between 1980 and 2000) are the biggest generation of buyers on the planet at present, and have the highest purchasing power due to this. They are the same generation who turned adults around September 11, 2001,, and began their careers into their careers following the Great Recession. This means that people between the ages of 15 and 35 are living in an economic climate that is different from generations before. But today's Digital Age offers many more opportunities to earn income to those imaginative and ambitious. They are also committed to earning what some think of as non-traditional income that is which isn't linked to a 9-5 work schedule. According to numerous reports the internet is expected to generate more millionaires during this generation than the stock market.

Chapter 7: The Value of Credit Score

If you aren't able to come up with the money or cash to purchase something for cash like a car, or a home You can seek credit, typically through a bank. It's similar to a loan they provide you with which has to be paid back with interest at a later date. Of of course, banks do not give loans to anyone. The bank must ensure that the borrower can be trusted to repay the loan in the future. To determine that, the bank typically examines the credit history of the individual.

A credit score that is good is a crucial factor in your daily life as it is basically evidence that you're in good shape with your finances and you have a track record of repaying your loans in time. With a credit score that is high you'll have no problems with any of the things that are listed below:

1.) Personal Relations: Yes, relationships shouldn't be forged by relying on money. However, it's difficult to argue that money does not play a part in the overall success of a relationship or marriage. Research has proven that money is the top reason couples go through divorced in marriage.

2.) Buy a Home A house purchase is a crucial decision since it's one of the most beneficial investments you can invest in your future. You can count on the value of your home to increase or lease your home to earn an income from passive sources. It is difficult to acquire in the event of a poor credit score.

3.) Find a job 3) Find a Job: This may be unfamiliar to you, however employers are now conducting credit checks on applicants for employment. This is typically seen in the federal sector, where the hiring requirements are more strict.

4.) How to Get a Loan As of right now banks are willing to provide loans to people with bad credit scores due to their financial need. But, the process might not be as simple even if you have an excellent credit. The interest rate on your loan is likely to be higher than normal.

Maintaining a good credit score will help you save cash on the high interest rates.

What is the method used to calculate credit scores?

There are two major types of scoring system available:

1.) FICO Score - The range of FICO score is between 300 and 850. A typical FICO score is around 689.

2.) Vantage Score The three credit bureaus TransUnion, Experian and Equifax came together to offer an alternative to the FICO score. While the same formula can be employed by all three credit agencies however, the Vantage Score is different due to the fact that each company taps into various databases.

The idea behind scoring is much simpler than it appears. In reality, they all employ a similar formula, and the differences in the scores are determined by their databases that contain different information.

The credit score derives by a mathematical formula that considers every aspect of your credit history, including your credit rating, your debt history, payment habits as well as your personal income and other variables. In addition, all of these elements depend on each other which makes it challenging to know what your credit score could come out.

The significance of credit in the present world is crucial and neglecting it can be extremely negative to your financial wellbeing. So, you must be aware of ways to ensure that your credit history is in good condition.

Chapter 8: What is Credit Score?

Credit is simply the ability to credit. Therefore your credit score can be described as an indicator of the risk that a lender is facing if they decide to loan money to you. It is determined by the study of your credit history and files. A different definition of credit is that it's the difference between refusing credit and receiving. Because the availability of money is usually limited and therefore, borrowing is a good alternative to get money to accomplish whatever you wish to accomplish. It lets you take on tasks that you might be unable to afford paying cash. Credit score is a measure of how lenders see your credit score when they advance funds to you; when your score is excellent indicates that you're an honest borrower, so you will not have to pay more. However, if the score is low the lenders will treat the borrower with caution and will cost you more money to extend the credit. What you pay for the borrowing (interest that you have to pay) is typically correlated with your score on credit. In other words, your credit score decides the amount you are required to pay for mortgage insurance for your car, health insurance, and a host of other items like phone, utilities and car payment. Employers also examine the credit score of their employees before making a hiring decision and this could determine whether you're employed or not. As you will see, If your credit score is not excellent, your life could be a complete nightmare. It's likely that you won't imagine living in the dream home of your dreams or driving the dream car as these is impossible. In essence your credit score will eventually determine what kind of lifestyle you have.

The type of data used to score your credit
Generallyspeaking, the five areas which make up what is known as the FICO score.

*Payment history (35 percent) The lender would like to know if you make your payments to credit accounts in time. Many lenders appear to be nervous about the indicators of late payment. They anticipate the possibility of default and delinquent interactions with clients who are in this situation.

*Amounts due (30 30 percent) Accounts that have balances does not necessarily indicate that you're a poor borrower and have poor FICO scores. The majority of credit cards permit minimal payments to your account since the balance will be revolving. If you've handled your account efficiently and punctually there is nothing to worry about so regards your credit score in the matter of your score.

Longer credit history increases your score (15 15%) The reasoning behind this is that if you've had to borrow for a lengthy period of time, you are an excellent borrower, or you'd have been refused credit by the people who looked at your application. It is a myth that avoiding credit is beneficial in terms of your credit rating. This is a false assumption. The lenders need to know what you do with credit prior to deciding whether they want to engage you. If you don't manage credit, there's no way of knowing what might take place; you may also be considered a high chance. It's often misinterpreted to suggest that you shouldn't take out loans due to the fact that you cannot pay.

It is also possibility to get a limited credit history, but still score very well on FICO.

A few important elements that are to be considered are:

*The kinds of credit available for use (10 percent): FICO also considers the combination of retail accounts, installment loans as well as mortgage loan.

*New credit (10%)-The age of your accounts Your age, which is the age of your account with the oldest balance and that of the most recent account are considered. They also consider that the age average of each account is taken into consideration. The time it's been since you last used the account are also taken into consideration.

Please note that your personal and demographic data like where you're from, your race or preference (religious or other) will not impact your score on credit. A credit score that is high can allow you to get credit at less cost.

The reason for Credit Scores

Credit scores are created to limit various kinds of risk. The most often cited danger is that of loaning money to the borrower. It is a measure of creditworthiness i.e. whether lending money to you is dangerous. Also, a credit score is a method to assess the risk of credit. It was developed in the midst of a method of giving credit to borrowers was incongruous slow, inefficient, and unfairly biased. Here's a quick summary of the reasons credit scoring is fantastic.

Credit scores help people receive loans more quickly (almost instantaneously) because lenders can speed up approval processes. The ability to get immediate credit decisions if are a lender. That means that borrowers can gain access to credit quickly.

It is an objective method of making credit decisions It is based on facts rather than emotions that are not substantiated.

There are a few credit errors The scoring takes in consideration a variety of factors, thus giving fair credit to those who have a negative credit history.

Credit is more plentiful: Lenders approve more loans on the basis of credit.

#Lower rates on credit The number of lenders (credit) which means more competition, which pushes the cost of credit to a lower level.

Credit scores are available from your credit file. There are numerous methods for scoring credit scores in the USA. But, the most widely employed method is called the FICO score which is a range of 300-850 The higher the rate greater the credit and the reverse goes for. The three FICO scores that are generated by the various credit report bureaus, with the three major ones being Experian, TransUnion and Equifax.

Then, why do you need to maintain your credit score? Here are some reasons you should strive to keep the credit score you have as good as it can be.

What are the reasons why your credit score should be so high?

A lower cost of credit: Lenders are more likely to give an interest rate that is lower. Here's a real-world scenario:

The credit score of 750 can translate into the equivalent of a 6.11 interest rate on a 30-year year mortgage of $300,000, whereas an average score of 620 amounts to an 7.42 interest rate on that same loan. You can clearly see that this distinction can easily translate to hundreds of dollars over the 30 year mortgage time.

This places you on the same level with lenders and creditors. It is easy to negotiate in the knowledge that lenders are competing to get you as a safe lender.

Furthermore, businesses are attracted to your business due to it being an asset of high value because due to the risk-free.

Insurance companies may also ask for your credit history prior to making decisions about your insurance premiums, or whether they'll take on the risk you take.

Let me explain first the way the credit system works in order to help you understand why credit ratings are a problem and the reasons why it's so hard keeping your credit score up to par.

Chapter 9: Create A Plan

"When an individual does not know the harbor he's taking,

"No wind is the right wind."

* Seneca

Author's note In this chapter, we will look at the crucial importance of establishing and keeping the budget. For step by step instructions the "Credit Friendly Budget Guide" is available at: www.FinancialEmpowermentServices.com/credit-friendly/

If you don't plan, you're guaranteed to achieve it.

Do you have any hopes for the future?

Do you want to make more cash?

Do you want to travel?

Do you want to be able spend time with your loved ones and family

Everybody says "yes" in these kinds of questions. We all have hopes dreams, aspirations and hopes. And if you ask these questions with another that asks "Have previously set any goals to make these goals come true?" - many people claim you have. But If you inquire "Have you planned for any of this?" - the answer is usually "no".

"Budget" is the term of universal fear. The majority of Americans don't plan nor manage their expenses on a monthly basis however the reasons aren't well identified, here are the principal reasons I've learned through conversations with clients throughout my career:

"I spend every penny I earn each month and I don't have enough funds to plan my budget."

"I am able to earn sufficient money in order to pay for my expenses, and I don't have to set up a budget."

"A budget acts as shackle that robs me of my choice to decide what and when I use my funds."

"The budget I have in my mind is good enough."

"It's too much trouble."

All of them sound reasonable. They may even contain elements of truth. But the reality is that for the majority of us, they are excuses to avoid facing the brutal realities of our financial practices. Let's look at each separately:

It's a myth that says: "I don't have enough funds to plan my budget."

If you're barely scraping by each month but do not spend a dime on extravagant purchases, it's easy to question the importance of a budget. This is why this argument is so effective. Why should you plan out what you'll spend your money on when everything is already budgeted? The truth is that setting priorities and creating the discipline required to adhere with a plan are the abilities that allow one to move beyond a pay check to paycheck life and reach financial wealth.

It's a myth that says: "I make enough money I don't need to plan my budget."

This is yet another widely believed argument that conceals two distinct concerns:

One of them is the notion that maybe I don't earn enough money. We've all been able to live beyond our means through attempting to make up the gap through credit cards, advances on our payroll, or simply not paying our bills. While acknowledging this isn't easy however, the advantage of knowing the truth about our situation is significant.

The third concern is the fear of failing. In the words of best-selling author Jim Collins wrote: "Good is not the same as Great." In the case of those who live in a comfortable or perhaps barely passable, why would you risk the risk? The reason for this can only be discovered by the person you are. What is it that would be the best thing that you could do to make your life better? Are you determined to achieve that goal?

Myth: "A budget strips me of my liberties." This is among my most favorite reasons, as it's probably true. There's an element of freedom removed when you limit your spending by setting budgets. However, it's not as easy.

The process of budgeting is a "free" choice. We make the decision to budget, not in order to be a burden on ourselves, but rather to create a path to an even higher level of financial independence and the more freedoms which come with it.

Furthermore, many purchases we justify by arguing that they are free are not as secure as we imagine. The most common use of this argument is to justify impulse purchases, which aren't otherwise easy to justify.

Budgeting is not a way to end freedom, it just frees us from the shackles of our minds. By budgeting, you can design your own way to financial freedom!

It's a myth that says: "I keep it in my mind."

When I was a student, this seemed like a perfect logical argument. Like many university students, I was on an ATM budget. If the ATM offered me funds, "yay." If there was no money, "darn." If you're struggling to live to the penny each month any variation of the ATM budget may work for you , too. However, it's really an attempt to cover any and all previous concerns.

Additionally, the head is the main source for the majority of our impulse purchases.

It's a lot easier to justify purchases with quick and easy mental games. The head is not a safe spot to store one's spending.

A budget isn't just being aware of how much money is on the books in the banking. It is a process of setting goals. By budgeting, you set the priorities of your lifestyle and develop an action plan to implement them. If you're concerned about the future of your family, then write it down.

Myth: "It's too much hassle."

This is definitely one of the most genuine arguments. It's much more difficult to make a budget rather than ignoring it. But, the significant impact that it has on your life budgets is enough to warrant the effort required to make it.

So , how do you budget?

It's a straightforward procedure. In its simplest form, we calculate our after tax income and subtract it from our monthly expenses. The difficulty lies in prioritizing expenditures. The categories we employ to achieve this goal were first introduced in the previous chapter:

- Mandatory Costs
- - Savings
- Considered and carefully considered desires
- Non-crucial Desires
- Expenses that are not necessary
Unnecessary Fees
Personal investment

If you conduct an extensive expense review using chapter 3, you'll be able to determine your current expenses. Start now by recording for one month, every purchase , and keep track of the expense all in one location. The act of recording your expenses increases your knowledge of them.

Once you've identified the issues the next step is to make your choices. Your expenses must be in line with your income. If they aren't, you'll require a boost in your earnings or cut down on your expenses. To achieve this, you might discover after careful consideration that your desires that aren't essential aren't necessary and your meticulously contemplated desires aren't as vital as you believed they would be.

There are some healthy habits you should consider:

First, pay yourself. Once your obligatory expenses have been identified, you can transfer a portion of your income into savings, preferably 10% if you are able. If you think that's too much you can reduce it to a lower amount. Make sure you are saving a certain amount every month.

Eliminate one habit that isn't necessary every month. If it's drinking a lot of soda or dining out more often Focus on changing one negative habit each month.

Create the habit of being thrifty. The process of cutting down on spending doesn't have to be a burden. Although it is against the norms of our society to buy shiny and new searching for deals can be enjoyable, and even when you change the way you view it.

There are many tools available to assist you in budgeting. If you're comfortable with computers, you can utilize budget templates already designed or created by others or make your own using these popular spreadsheet applications:

- Microsoft Excel

Open Office Spreadsheet Spreadsheet

-- Google Doc Spreadsheet

If you prefer using the pencil or paper option, visit the local office supply stores to find budgeting sheets. You can get an online version of the Credit Friendly Budget Guide mentioned at the beginning of this chapter.

Keep it up!

It's a lot of work. However, it's the most important task that one can take on for their financial future. Budgeting is more than just the details of spending each month. Budgeting is an essential aspect in establishing your life's goals. It shouldn't be an exercise in drudgery and should be an opportunity to look into your desires and determine the routes to get there.

Recommendations to help you make an Action Plan:

1. Don't believe the myths that stop you from making a budget. The advantages of budgeting surpass any arguments not to.

2. Be sure to evaluate your thoughtfully considered and non-essential goals. The vast majority of money allocated in these groups could effectively used elsewhere.

3. The first step is to budget towards true financial maturity. Create an annual budget. Follow it. Be a conscious person.

Chapter 10: Things You Should Not Do After You Have Fixed Your Credit

We've discussed the things are you able to do to fix your credit score, In this section, we will look at the actions are not recommended as they will only increase your score on credit.

Without a plan

If you embark on your journey without a plan, you're likely to make a mistake. Don't make a decision without a plan since it will be extremely difficult. When you are ready to begin fixing your credit, make an action plan for yourself. Try to stick to it until you're done. It is possible to begin by writing down the obligations and the funds you have, and then shift towards determining the amount you need to save up to pay it off in full. This way, you'll avoid wasting cash and will be able to pay off your debts more quickly.

Paying bills late

One of the most unwise actions you can commit is fail to pay the bills in time. You may think you can save money by making late payments, but it's an untrue assumption. Keep in mind the fact that 35% of your credit score is comprised of your payment history. Anything that you do not pay on time or fail to pay can lower your credit score considerably. If you'd want to, you can download an app that reminds you of when to pay your bill each month. Make sure to pay it on the day of the bill of the month to ensure you aren't tempted to forget it later.

The cost of borrowing a large loan

If you're already suffering from financial stress due to poor credit, you shouldn't increase the stress by taking out an enormous loan. The loan could be used intended for your personal use or as a way to clear outstanding debts. However, if you weren't able to pay back the debts you incurred from previous borrowings and you're not in a position to repay it with this loan. Don't fall for the temptation to make a loan from lenders or banks, which could charge you high interest rates, and also cause harm for your credit.

A firm that can help

If you think the company is keen to assist you without charging a substantial sum for their services If you think that they will, then you are wrong. Every company is trying to get every day more cash out of you. This can put you in a compromising situation. And if they are providing services for free and is not a legitimate business, it may not be a sound suggestion you are being offered. Don't be rushed to get the services of a business at the beginning. Give it some time and then do everything you can to fix your credit. If you are still not occurring, you may contact them.

Making use of credit cards to spend

It is not something you need is to make use of your credit card and purchase all the nice and costly items. Many will believe that it's not good to spend money on something because it could impact their social standing. This thought can result in a negative impact on your score on credit. It will result in a score that could lead that you lose all your card completely and never have the possibility of applying for an alternative. So, you should be able to control your desires to spend and reduce the amount you spend whenever possible.

Distress sale

If you've got a low score, it is not a good idea to be a maniac and sell anything that is important to you to make enough money. It is possible that you will suffer losses as a result. You could instead hang the item in your possession and take out a loan from someone you know or a family member. If the cost of the item increases then you can offer it to raise money, and then repay the amount you borrowed, and retain the remainder as your earnings.

Filing for bankruptcy

The filing of bankruptcy should not be your first choice. You should resist any desires to file for bankruptcy and, even if told to do so take a look at alternatives. It is possible to seek financial advice and learn how to lower your debts and get you out of a bad credit score. If you have filed for bankruptcy at least once, you'll find it very difficult to get a new credit score again, and you will not have the option of eradicating the bankruptcy mark from the score of your credit.

Removing old cards

Never cancel your oldest cards. If you must do so, then you need to close your most recent credit cards. If you do this for old cards and then be able to erase a large portion of your payment history off your credit report and cutting it down. This will not be a good thing since you may have been able to make timely payments in the past and your record on the card may be good.

Maintaining track

Inadequately tracking your movements could be a bad thing to do. Therefore, you must be aware of every move. Keep a log and note down your expenses, your payment or borrowings, and so on. So, you'll know exactly where you are at any point in time, and be able to refer back to you to review whenever you are you are asked by a banker or creditor.

Chapter 11: Keep Track Of Bills

One of the most significant issues that many people face in getting their credit back to where it should be is paying the bills in time. What can you do to fix it? The best thing you can be making reminders to notify you of when your bills have to be paid, and the amount you have to pay for each one. Reminders is something you notice, and it is something you can address quickly.

What that means is that you need a signal like an alarm. It's something you shouldn't avoid and you have to investigate right away. Most people write on their calendars just does not work, or placing notes on their refrigerator won't work. Set an alarm in your phone or set your alarm to go off at a particular time every day when you must pay a bill, the alarm sounds. In the event of an alarm, write down the reason it is to be used for. (Pay your utility bill, for instance.) This is how you can ensure that the task gets completed.

Another aspect to consider while setting the alarm clock is whether you'll be in a position to handle the issue immediately. If you aren't able to deal with the issue promptly, you're not doing your part to help yourself. The alarm should be set to sound at a time that you are able to log onto an online computer to make the payment , or sit down and write the check. If you are forced put it off until later (for instance when you return home) it's likely that you'll forget about it and defeat the whole reason for setting an alarm.

Of course, for this to be effective, all, you need to be aware of what your bills cost and when they'll be due. Make time to look through your bills. Sort them according to the due date which is on the sheet of paper. Write down all of your bills with the due date, the minimum amount of payment and the amount due to be paid. Use that information to add the bill along with the amount due in your phone , so that an alarm will sound on the day that the due date. This will allow you to have the time to deliver the bill to the mail (or pay it via the web) one day prior to the time the due date. If you mail the bill with a postmark, it will be considered to have been paid on time once it reaches the office.

Also, make sure to create a notification on your smartphone to go to the exact time each month. This will make sure that it doesn't keep repeating and you can keep track of what you have to do and when to complete it. It is not necessary to pay the minimum amount on all your cards, however knowing what the minimum amount is will make it easier so that you don't search for the payment. You'll be able review the notification and immediately make the payment.

Chapter 12: Maintaining A Great Credit Score for Life

If you are able to push your FICO score above the 720 mark, it's crucial to know how to keep it up. It is also crucial to realize that your score can fluctuate. This is the reason it is essential to keep an eye on your credit score for any significant changes.

If a negative entry appears in your report, make sure you pay it right away, in the majority of cases, you'll receive around 80% of the points which were lost the moment the report is posted as paid. The remaining 20% will be returned over the course of a 12 month period. It's always a good idea to phone call to ask the creditor if they'd be willing to erase the account from the report. Some might agree, while others might say they aren't able to.

Keep your revolving credit in good standing. I can't stress enough how much importance the revolving credit has on your credit score. Never close your oldest account. Keep in mind that at the start of this book , it was mentioned that the duration of your credit accounts can be a significant part of your overall score. This may not sound like a lot, but your score is ranging between 300 and 850. If you calculate the total of 550 points, 15% could be as high as an 83-point portion of your score. Again, let me reiterate, never close your oldest account!

Make sure that all payments are made on time. If they report to the bureau, it's crucial to ensure that the payment isn't more than more than 30 days late. This credit score system isn't solely based on late payments. So if your due date is due on 1st, and isn't paid by the 15th, it might not be timely to the lender however it won't be reported as late to credit bureaus until the date it has been late for 30 days. The credit bureaus report 30-60 90, 120, and 150-day late payment. Naturally, any of these could destroy your credit quite quickly.

A 30-day payment that is late could affect your score by 60 to 75 points. These points are hard to recover and must be restored over time. If you find that a late or missed payment is a very unusual occurrence and you are able to prove it, then you might be able to get it taken away. There's a certain language that you must use when speaking to your creditor. The majority of creditors when asked to remove late payments will reply "no" due to the fact that they don't know they are in a position to remove late payments. If you contact them and ask whether they'll remove that late fee, you can ask them to make an "goodwill adjustment". This is the phrase they will need to be able to appreciate the capability. If they're not able or unwilling to assist, it's important to ask their supervisor.

Make sure to keep the balances on your credit accounts under 25 percent of your limit. Utilize them for a couple of months and make sure you pay your debts. This improves your score in nearly all aspects of credit scores, including the history of your payments, the amount due, the duration of credit accounts and credit utilization.

Be careful about your credit limit will accept and do not open more than one account within a short time. Remember that 10 percent part of your credit score built on new credit. The phrase "new credit" is often confused. This section considers all inquiries and new credit. I'm sure all of us are aware of the fact that inquiries can lower your score. So having multiple accounts and inquiries can reduce your score in the 10% mark.

Chapter 13: Student Loan Relief Programs

We are currently in a tough economy , and people are having more difficulty than ever to pay their student loans. A lot of Americans have two jobs in order to survive, and many of the newest graduates are having a difficult time to find work in their chosen field of study.

What can you do if having trouble making your payments on student loans?

Student loans are beneficial in helping to establish an outstanding credit score. they are considered an instalment account or trade line on your credit due to the fact of the fixed amount, therefore you need to make every effort to not make a late payment of your loan. If you are experiencing financial difficulties it is possible that you are qualified for deferment or the option of forbearance for your federal loans. This allows you to temporarily delay or decrease your monthly payments and will help you avoid getting into the position of being in default on your student loans.

Deferment is a time during which the repayment of principal and interest on your loan are temporarily deferred. Deferment is granted in certain situations like unemployment, a minimum income, or being in the military or in the in the community. Contact Financial aid of the institution you attend and also your lender. They will send you the necessary documentation to submit the deferment application.

Forbearance happens when you're given permission by your lender to cease making payments or reduce the amount of your monthly payments for the federal loans you have taken out for up 12 months. It is an option in the event that you're not eligible for deferment, but through a forbearance agreement, you will be charged interest on both the loans that are subsidized or unsubsidized. Mandatory forbearances may be granted to:

Participating in a medical or dental residency or dental internship.

The amount you must pay each month on all student loans that you've received is at least 20% of your monthly income.

National service post in which you have been awarded an award of national service.

Teaching services that are eligible for loan forgiveness for teachers.

You can be eligible to repay a portion of your loans through the U.S. Department Of Defence Student Loan Repayment Program.

You are an employee of the National Guard and have been appointed by the governor, however you aren't qualified for a military deferment

Deferred payments are more beneficial over forbearance on federal student loans due to the interest charged by the federal government. Forbearance is a second alternative to delaying your payment. Once you've been accepted for a deferment, or forbearance, you will keep paying your student loans, unless you are instructed otherwise. Your credit score will not be affected by either of these options, and it will remain to provide you with an excellent credit score.

PAYE Program

The Pay as You Earn program is a federally-funded program that was enacted into law in December 2012. This was the very first law to ease student debt that was signed by the President Barack Obama. Students who have student loans must be able to prove that their loans were made available after October 1st 2007 and must have had at least one loan disbursement prior to October 1, 2011. In addition, the 10-year standard repayment amount cannot exceed 10 percent of individual's discretionary income.

Benefits of Programs
* The program keeps the costs low during the initial stages of the loan, and then increases to keep pace with the increase in salary.
* Following 20 years of paying, there will be a loan forgiveness.

Certain borrowers who decide to go into public service will be able to have their debt forgiven in just 10 years.

The government is responsible for an unpaid interest rate in the case of Direct Subsidized Loans and on the portion that is subsidized of Direct Consolidation Loans for three years in the event that your loan amount is not enough to cover the interest. In addition, interest capitalization is not a given to a certain extent, including deferment and forbearance, so long as the individual who is borrowing is in compliance with the requirements for hardship.

Program weaknesses

They'll look at the amount of debt in relation to salary, so that eligibility and payments are dependent on the household's income, not to the individual's income. For married borrowers, one whose spouse earns about the same amount, however has no debts outstanding from student loans may not gain anything at all.

The borrower could be required to pay taxes on forgiven portions of loans as soon as it is in the forgiveness amount. It is important to save the amount to pay the tax.

Participants must present evidence of eligibility each year.

The borrower who is a part of the program will be charged more in total interest because of the lengthening duration of repayment time.

This program is applicable only to federal loans. Federal Direct Loans are not eligible, but the other loans for students are also taken into consideration when determining the hardship. Federal Family Education Loans or (FFEL) loans aren't suitable for this plan however, they are taken into consideration when eligibility is established. FFELs can be used to qualify for income-based Repayment plans.

Remember, If the loan amount is enough to last for 20 years, the total will remain the same regardless of how large the amount.

REPAYE Program

President Obama recently issued a memorandum to facilitate to expand the PAYE Program to 5 million more customers. It is believed that the Revised PAYE Program (also known as (REPAYE) may be in place by either in late 2015 or the beginning of 2016. The revisions made to REPAYE will permit low income loans, but will limit the amount of high-income borrowers who could be tempted to take advantage of these attractive terms for payment.

Benefits of the program

The program will be available to all borrowers that have Federal Direct Loans, no regardless of the loan's initial date.

Older loans that have been financed can be combined to qualify for.

No income requirements

No financial hardship proof is needed.

The program's payment is equal to 10% of loan discretionary income.

Forgiveness of loans in 20 years for undergraduates

Forgiveness of loans for 25 years for graduates

The program restricts the amount of amount of interest charged to the borrower when the when the amount of the payment is not enough to cover the interest for the month. The borrower will be paid half of the interest they pay that month and the Government will be responsible the remainder of the interest on the borrower's.

Program weaknesses

They'll consider the amount of debt in relation to salary, so the eligibility for loans and the payment limits are dependent on the household's income, not to individuals' income. If you are a married borrower one whose spouse earns about the same amount however has no debts outstanding from student loans they may not gain anything at all.

The borrower might have to pay taxes on forgiven portions of loans as soon as it is in the forgiveness amount. It is important to save the amount for the tax payment.

There is no limit on the amount the loan can be increased to when the borrower's income increases.

You need to re-certify your household's income and size or be included under the "Alternate plan".

Options for repayment based on income

The Income-Based Repayment (IBR) Plans are availableand dependent on 15 % of the borrower's discretionary income. There are also other options for repayment that may extend repayment plans as well as graduated repayment plans, where payments begin low, but rise every two years the duration of up to 25 years, to ensure that the repayments are reasonable. FFELs cannot be qualified for this program, however the borrower can combine FFELs to directly into the Direct Loan program. The loan should have been established on or before October 1, 2007.

Help for Student Loans that Are in Default

We have discussed in the beginning chapters how defaulting on your student loan could cause financial ruin. A few of those reading this book are in this same situation however there is hope. There are two main options available to federal student loans that are in default are loans rehabilitation and consolidation.

Program for loan rehabilitation

The program requires the person who is in default, to pay on-time payments. The payments are based on the borrower's earnings against their expenses. The borrower is required to pay nine monthly installments on or before the date due in the period of 10 months consecutive. After the borrower has completed the monthly payment plan, the loan will be released of default. The lender will apply IBR to calculate the IBR formula for loans that are older and also on the borrower who is making monthly payments to a student loan equal to 15% of disposable income. It does not mean you can qualify to receive IBR even if you're in default. Instead, the holder of the loan uses the 15 percent IBR formula to calculate the most reasonable and affordable amount. If you can successfully repair this loan may apply for one that is based on income.

Program benefits

There is no longer a chance for you to be considered to be in default by the lender you have in your credit file.

No more garnishments on your earnings.

They will stop accepting your tax returns for income

You'll be eligible to be eligible for federal student loans and federal grants once more.

You could qualify with a VA and HUD loan

Remember that you're entitled to exit default by rehabilitation just once for each loan. If you had rehabilitated student loans prior to the 14th of August, 2008 and fall back into default for the loan, you are able to continue to rehab, but it is dependent on the one-time limit.

There are also collection charges payable to collection agencies. From July 1st, 2014, this is not more than 16% of the outstanding principal and accrued interests when you sell selling of the loan.

The program of loan consolidation

This requires you to make voluntary regular payments to the borrower's earnings versus their expenses over three consecutive, reasonable and affordable monthly payments , or agreeing to pay in accordance with the Income Contingent Repayment (ICRP) or Income Based Repayment (IBR) plan. This is the most efficient method however credit won't be restored and you'll be liable for collections charges that could increase your debt by up to 25 percent.

Consolidating federal loan debt into private consolidation loans will result in the loss of your rights under loans that are offered by the federal government. This includes deferment, forgiveness cancellation, deferment, and the right to repay federal loans.

Private Student Loans

A private student loan, also known as another loan can be described as a private loan to fund education. Repayment terms differ between private lenders, however certain private lenders provide flexible repayment terms as well as impressive consolidation loans that can ease difficulties with repayment, and deferment for private loans is determined on the basis of a case-by-case basis.

If you're having issues in dealing with your lenders, you can reach them at the Department of Education ombudsman office at

U.S. Department of Education

FSA Ombudsman Group

830 First Street, N.E., Mail Stop 5144

Washington, DC 20202-5144

Phone: 1-877-557-2575

Fax: 202-275-0549

The Consumer Financial Protection Bureau also offers a private student loan Ombudsman office, as well as other offices services to assist with resources for student loans.

Phone: 855-411-2372

To process a online complaint on the Consumer Financial Protection Bureau website

http://www.consumerfinance.gov/complaint/

Chapter 14: How Can I get rid of This Negative Item?

There are still ways to remove this negative entry from your credit history, without impacting your credit score.

1. Goodwill Removal

Similar to a goodwill adjust request for payment that is late, you could also utilize a goodwill cancellation request the moment that your account is in the point of collection. This may sound as if it's a big risk however it's worth it. You'll need to create a goodwill letter to your lender asking them to forgive the late payment. Then, you can ask that your account be included into their automatic payment system in the event that they have one to ensure that your lender will believe that you're sincere when apologize. It is possible to request one especially if the debt has been paid in full.

2. Dispute your account if it isn't supposed to be in Collections

If you feel that the amount owed by the agency that collects your debts isn't yours, then you should take every step to remove it. There is no obligation to pay it, and collection agencies are not permitted to put it on your credit reports. However in the event that you are the owner of the debt and the debt collector has been contacting you for the initial 30 days after it was incurred, then you can ask for a debt validation before proceeding with any other actions. If they don't respond to your request, there is no need to take action. If they did, and you find that the information was incorrect or is related to a debt of someone else You can dispute the information and present any evidence that shows the information they provided was not correct.

3. Pay for removal

If your dispute isn't running smoothly, but you wish to eliminate the issue as soon as you can at the earliest time, and are willing to pay a certain amount so that your collection agency can remove the item from your credit report, then you are able to pay them off. This is a good option for collections that are incorrect or correct however you don't have patience to sit and wait on your bank to get the debt removed, likely due to a loan or card application you wish to submit an application for within the coming weeks. The process of paying for deletion doesn't necessarily mean you're willing to pay the amount they're requesting from you. It's just to get the item removed to ensure that it doesn't appear upon your credit file. If you decide to do this ensure that you get your collector to sign an agreement note in the amount you paid them. It should be specifically stating that you desire that the item be removed from your credit report and not to settle any balances.

Collection agencies often respond to this demand by saying that they can't erase the negative information. And often, that is the case. The credit reporting agencies have agreements with prohibit this kind of activity, or else everyone are able to alter their creditworthiness. If, however, things turn to worse and your lender refuses the request to pay for removal then you'll have to pay off the balances and keep them until the time limit for negative items to expire.

4. A dispute after 7 years

According to FCRA A past due account or collection item may remain on your credit report just seven years after the date of first delinquency So if it lingers more than seven years, you are able to at any time request its removal or, if it is not requested, it will be removed by default.

Some credit collection agencies will attempt to make your debt appear older by making it appear like the debt was delinquent for longer than it actually been. This can keep the negative record on your credit report for a bit longer. If you believe that the seven-year reporting period has ended in full, you have the rights to challenge the report and get that item taken off.

It doesn't mean that your balances that are not paid must be wiped out too. Collectors may still call the customer to pay your debts but the negative charge must be removed.

Credit Inquiries

If you take it literally In its most literal sense, an Credit Inquiry is an inquiry made by the business or the institution you applied for a loan or service, or for money from. It could be a bank to which you used a credit card to or mortgage, car loans and , sometimes, companies you have applied for a job. It is also possible to see inquiries from businesses you don't know about. The only inquiries that will contribute to your Vantage Score or FICO are those that result from the new credit applications you have made.

When your FICO scores are affected They are likely to not be much lower. If you are applying for several credit cards within a brief time frame, multiple requests will show up on your credit report. Applying for credit for the first time can be considered a higher risk but the majority of credit scores aren't affected by multiple requests from mortgage, auto or student loan companies within an extremely short time. Most of the time, these inquiries are seen as one-time inquiries and can have a slight impact on your credit score.

If a consumer has applied for credit cards several times within the span of a few months the only thing that happens is to mean that the institutions or banks which he has applied to are unable to pay their credit limit at the lowest This will be reflected in a number of inquiries to the credit history of the person. For the majority of people, an additional credit inquiry can earn less than five points off the FICO Score. If you are looking for An outlook report, the entire range of FICO Scores is between 300 and 850. It is possible that inquiries will have a larger impact if you only have few accounts or an unproven credit history. Large numbers of inquiries result in higher risk. According to research, those with at least six inquiries on their credit reports could be as much as eight-fold more likely declare bankruptcy than those with zero inquiries on their report. The results of inquiries often be a factor in the assessment of risk, but they play only a small part. Other important elements that affect your score are the speed at which you pay your debts and the overall burden of debt reported in your credit score.

Usually, the total amount of the credit inquiries made is listed at the bottom or the last section on your Credit Report.

When you get a paper copy of your report credit reports, there is an inquiry section made on your account exactly like those on the TransUnion samples of credit file, which will usually be located on the bottom of the report. The section will show the names of the companies that have requested your information to examination. It will also give you the date the request was made and the phone number of the company or reference. Certain of these companies might not be familiar to you due to the fact that those companies who made the request could be a third-party company that is employed by the institution you submitted an request for credit or a loan to.

It is vital to be aware that your credit report will differ according to the institution which sent the report to. For instance, a specific bank you held one of their accounts for fifteen years and was the first to grant you a credit card as a result of your reliability and consistency in saving could be sending your credit report to Experian. This report could ensure you a good score. In another business you may have experienced an incident where you had one or two payment that was late and the report is sent to TransUnion. There is a chance that your credit report receive might come from TransUnion and the score may not be as good. There is a major three credit bureaus it's worth knowing which one gets the report and, if not, you can simply request the account of all the credit bureaus.

Different types of inquiries

There are a few inquiries about credit that show up within your credit reports can have an adverse effect on your credit score. Certain inquiries aren't necessary and the bank or the company that you're applying for an loan to will not require. There are two kinds of inquiries: the soft inquiry as well as the harder inquiry. A hard inquiry is the only one that can affect your credit score negatively However, certain inquiries won't affect the score.

1. Soft Inquiry Soft inquiries are credit checks which do not have your credit examined by a prospective lender. It is one type of inquiry that occurs when your company might want to conduct a background check for you or when you are granted a pre-approval to the use of credit cards or similar activities. Another scenario is that you are checking your credit score by using a different platform, or any other way you'd like to verify it. These kinds of inquiries can occur without your knowledge, but not like the case of a formal inquiry. They may or might not appear within your credit reports dependent on the credit bureau that is providing the report. 2. Hard Inquiry - Hard inquires are credit checks in which a potential creditor is looking into your credit history because you've made an

application for credit from them, and this is typically an authorized review of your credit score. One example is applying for the loan of a house, car, mortgage, loan, student loan or credit card. A single application counts as an inquiry. For certain credit bureaus, one inquiry can be considered to be not more than five points in your score. A notable exception however there is the so-called Rate Shopping.

What is Rate Shopping?

The creditor will approve the need for money based on the particulars of each borrower, therefore there isn't a standard rate for the loan you can obtain through the institution. Different institutions or banks will give you various rates, while some provide you with a greater amount than others, and for you to be aware of this, it is essential to examine each prospective banks' offers. This is why you must examine the process of credit applications to understand the maximum amount you could get should you be accepted even. This procedure involves seeking an approval by you (in other words"as per request of Customer') to conduct a background check on your credit and your payment history, also known as a credit report. Each institution which you have applied for to get a loan at will run a background search and each inquiry added to your score.

This was the problem in the past, when the the reasons to apply for to borrow money were not considered. However, with the help of technological advancements made by companies that provide us with this data rate shopping is now accepted. But, you must complete your rate shopping within an exact timeframe to be considered one. If, however, you are able to apply for say three home loans and two auto loans within the same time frame and are regarded as two different inquiries. Why? Because the applications for the same financial needs could be classified as one.

When to Rate Shop

Some scoring platforms (FICO, VanatgeScore, etc.) offer various timeframes to deciding whether an inquiry can be classified as rate shopping. Aspects such as the amount of the loan, the nature of the loan, and the timeframe of the debt repayment will be considered when determining whether or not the inquiry can be included in one. The rate shopping window typically ranges between 14-45 days. For instance, if you apply for three house loans within 14-20 days, that is considered to be Rate Shopping.

Also, note that loans for mortgages, student or car are not counted against your FICO scores within the first 30 days. After 30 days any inquiries related to those transactions may remain on your FICO score for up to two years.

When is Rate Shopping not applicable?

While major credit inquiries such as cars, student/educational or home loans may be included in one inquiry to shop rates However, credit Card applications can't.

Customers who apply for multiple credit cards within a very short period of time are deemed to be high-risk, and these inquiries will be counted. This could adversely affect your score on credit, specifically in the case of small credit history.

Limiting your Hard Inquiries to the very minimum

While it's easy as it might appear, rate shopping may not be as simple as it seems or appears. The process of applying for a particular type of loan will require waiting for a while, and then filling out the forms, calling and follow-ups. However, you'll benefit from rate shopping, particularly if you're just beginning to establish your credit score or planning to save for a big loan. Here are some tips you could consider:

* Request an loan within 14 to 45 days. It might be worthwhile asking your credit bureau regarding the timeframe they have set to shop rates, but in the event that you don't have time for this, you should make sure to limit your requests to 14 days. It could be a busy time for you for the next two weeks however it's better than having

more inquiries that be on your credit report for two years.

* You can apply for one kind of loan at the same time in this manner, Strategies to Rebuild Your Credit Score

* Make the amount for each loan to the same amount. So, the loans you take out won't be misinterpreted as another type of loan when you need to inquire.

Bankruptcy

In the words of Investopedia.com, "Bankruptcy is a legal proceeding that involves a or business who is unable to pay any outstanding debts. The bankruptcy process starts with the filing of a petition on behalf of the person who is in debt, and this process can be often filed and also on behalf on creditors' behalf however, this is not as common. All of the debtor's assets are measured and evaluated, and the assets may be used to repay a portion of outstanding debt." (Read more: Bankruptcy http://www.investopedia.com/terms/b/bankruptcy.asp#ixzz4kupSyOrj).

The filing of bankruptcy in a variety of ways can help you get an entirely new start with building your business, however this negative mark can remain in your credit record for a long period of time. Let's look at the benefits and negatives of the filing of Bankruptcy.

Negatives

While you're getting a fresh beginning to recover from your debts however, not all of it is going to be eliminated. The debts you'll remain even after filing bankruptcy include alimony, child support, your most recent tax bill and the student loan (most in the form of) and the fines you have to pay to authorities of the government.

* This negative mark stays in your credit record for 10 years and it will be a challenge to get credit cards or loans. If you do end up getting accepted, you'll have a greater chance of getting a higher interest rate.

* You'll lose all the exemptions on your property if you make an insolvency filing and, sometimes, based on your financial situation the properties you lose could be

your vehicle, stocks bonds, cash, or even your home.

It's costly to file for bankruptcy. you'll have to pay for many costs: bankruptcy costs, attorney's fees and fees for filing as well as trustees' fees counseling fees for credit and more.

Benefits

The filing of bankruptcy may assist you in getting rid of the majority all of the debts you owe (with being exempted from ones that are considered to be disadvantageous). That is you will no longer be in debt if you choose to file for bankruptcy.

If you're unable to make your payments You can request that they be legally canceled. It is also possible to make an application in Chapter 13 Bankruptcy, where you can organize your debts, and combine the debts into one monthly installment, and assist you in paying slowly but gradually.

* An automatic stay can also be issued, meaning those who owe money as well as creditors and other organizations are

barred from conducting any collection attempts through phone calls or emails, as well as other methods of communication.

* If you're worried about losing your entire belongings when you file bankruptcy do not be. The filing for Chapter 7 could permit you to keep some of your personal possessions, such as jewelry, clothing, home and other items that you consider personal. These are known as bankruptcy exemptions.

There are various types of bankruptcy filings. There are a variety of kinds of bankruptcy, however we will be discussing the two most commonly filed by individuals consumers.

How do I find Chapter 7?

Small and small-sized businesses or individuals are able to file for chapter 7 bankruptcy when they have no or enough non-exempt assets in order to pay off their debts , such as credit card charges, loans or other. Some of these non- exempt assets are stocks bonds, cash and high-value collections, as well as vehicles and homes. The consumers have to liquidate their non-exempt assets in order to repay their loans. If they do not, in the event that they do not have any assets with a specific value the debts are forgiven, that is, they won't be held accountable for the debts they owe.

How do I find Chapter 13?

This is a type of bankruptcy for those who have a high-value asset as compared to consumers who are eligible for chapter 7. In Chapter 13 bankruptcy, unlike Chapter 13 bankruptcy, individuals are able to arrange for a payment plan. And unlike Chapter 7, should an person come up with plans to settle their outstanding debts, the court might let them retain their assets, even non-exempt ones.

Can I still remove this Negative Item?

Despite the numerous online advertisements from major credit bureaus and other credit bureaus on the possibility of having a bankruptcy record be removed from your credit record the answer is yes. It is possible to request it be deleted on your own or seek assistance from credit repair firms.

Inquiring that your items of concern be taken care of on yourself can take up a lot the time as well as energy however it can be worthwhile. It is necessary to write an email to explain your request and maybe even make a call every now and then to you can follow up with them. If you aren't able to find the enough time to do this then you could always get assistance by a professional credit repair service.

TAX LIENS (both in the form of paid as well as non-paid)

If a tax-payer does not pay their tax in full, a tax lien is made through the federal government. This is a legal case of a government agency to the tax payer who has not paid. Tax liens are usually the last resort for collecting taxes from tax-payers who are not paying.

If taxes are still unpaid, the tax authority could make use of a tax levy to legally take possession of the assets of the taxpayer as payment. These include investments accounts, vehicles as well as real estate.

Tax liens are publically recorded and are reported to credit bureaus. If you have a tax lien report in your credit file the assets associated with the lien aren't sold. it also blocks the person from being approved for credit card applications, and other similar applications.

Is this item possible to remove?
In order to have the tax lien taken off your credit report the taxpayer has to pay back what you owe. Then, you can to get the debt released through bankruptcy court or negotiate an agreement with tax authorities. The federal and state governments could put tax liens on the non-paid tax owed to the federal government or for state taxes local governments may also place tax liens to collect unpaid local income or assets taxes. But, even if you pay our tax obligations, because tax liens are listed on public record, they could remain on your credit report for up to seven years after the date of the full payment.

Because the laws regarding lien can differ It is always wise to consult the appropriate sources, such as the IRS or the tax authority of your state or local authority and a tax attorney, or credit counselor. Be vigilant about your credit and manage it in good standing, since you're the only person who will reap the fruits of what you've sown.

Chapter 15: Ways To Repair A Bad

Credit Score

It's time to address an area of potential controversy for a few. This chapter will be devoted to the best ways to repair your credit score. A credit score can be worse than good. Perhaps you're only now looking into your credit score looks like and you're shocked to discover that your credit score isn't as you expected it to be. Perhaps you've experienced some tough circumstances lately and your credit score is suffering a setback that you're aware. Whatever the reason for arriving to this point, poor credit scores can have significant implications for other aspects in your daily life (which we've talked about in earlier chapters). If you've already made mistakes in earlier chapters and you're trapped in a position that you're desperate to get out of In this chapter, we'll give the necessary tips to achieve exactly that.

How Long Does It Take to Rebuild Your credit score?

Knowing the length of time it will take to fix your credit score can aid in providing you with more information but also motivate you to not making these kinds of mistakes. For the majority of actions that can lead to bad credit, the events will remain recorded on the credit reports for seven years. This includes the late payment, repossessions that have taken place in the past, foreclosures, short sales and tax lien. The only thing that can remain at the top of your report for longer than 7 years, is if you file for bankruptcy. The type of offense will be on your credit report for a whole decade. Being aware of the length of time your credit history is in your file brings the realization of how crucial it is to settle your credit debt promptly. The consequences, even if appear to be minor, can leave an long-lasting trail that is difficult to get rid of for the years to come. With these kinds of timelines in mind Let's glance at what steps you need to follow if you are looking to boost your bad credit score.

Step 1: Request your Credit Report Transcripts

To begin clearing your credit the initial step should be to obtain an account of your current credit reports. The report will reveal specific reasons for that your credit rating is getting worse and will help you determine what's going on in this report to fix it. It is not necessary to spend any money to get these reports. With the Fair Credit and Reporting Agency you're eligible to receive an unrestricted copy of your credit file each year. When you do this, it is important to collect your reports from all the top credit report agencies. In this way, you'll be able to determine the way each credit report is viewed by the lenders you decide to choose. It is impossible to determine what kind of credit an applicant is likely to use, therefore it is important to have all kinds of reports on credit to be accurate.

Step 2: How to Clean Your Credit Report

When you've got access to your credit reports It's not enough to just declare, "clean them up". It is important to understand how you can improve your credit report to make it look better. Let's examine the steps to take right now.

Tip 1. Finding the Mistakes

It may be a shock however, not all the information that appears on your credit reports is accurate. There may be errors. If you find any errors, you should contest the claims. You must dispute this transaction by contacting the account that initially placed the charges on your account. To accomplish this, you should either write to the company that is at issue or call their customer support phone number. Nowadays, a person will be available to assist you in the middle of the daytime.

Tip 2: Dispute the same claims on different Credit Reports

If you notice that the same errors appear on the different credit reports that you receive You will have to challenge every claim that appears on the various credit reports. It's not enough just to challenge the claim on one of your credit reports because the same mistakes could be present on other reports produced by you.

It can be a tedious task but it's well worth it at the end of the day.

Tip 3: Hiring an expert

Although you might be able to determine how to get rid of any mistakes on your credit report but you might not want to go through the effort of eliminating these mistakes by yourself. Law firms and credit repair companies are out there to deal with these issues for you. These firms aren't able to say that they will increase the credit rating of yours by any amount of points. They'll be honest and truthful with you. If they're not and believe they're not reliable Find aid somewhere else.

Step 3: Identify Positive Reinforcement

The secured credit card, as we've previously discussed have been specifically designed to assist people experiencing credit issues to solve their credit problems. If that you've had to turn down certain kinds of credit due to your previous actions, it doesn't mean you're in a bind. You can gradually improve your credit rating by taking advantage of this credit card. Like all credit cards it is necessary to establish better habits if are hoping to revive your credit rating.

The 4th Step: Be Consistent with Your Payments

It's crucial to not suggest that you're going through difficult times or have financial difficulties. To prevent this from happening you must, not only pay your credit cards in time, you should also make sure you pay a regular amount every month. If, for instance, you normally spend 2 hundred dollars a month on credit card bills but then you begin to pay fifty dollars, or even 25 dollars, your creditors will notice. Make sure you are consistent with your payments to make sure that your creditors aren't worried.

Step 5: Where to stay clear of using a Credit Card

As well as keeping your risk in check it is also important to avoid making use of your credit card in specific places like banks, pawnshops, or even with divorce attorneys. These kinds of locations indicate that you could be soon in a state of financial strain and that your creditors will reduce your credit score accordingly.

Chapter 16: Secured Credit Cards

How to Apply for a Secured Credit Card

What?? I know this goes against what I stated in Chapter 4. You'll find out what I'm talking about.

If someone is ready, begin applying for credit . . .

A secured credit card is a good way towards building a credit score if you have been denied credit on an ordinary credit card. It's not a requirement and many prefer against applying for secured credit cards. It's an option, and one to be considered cautiously before proceeding.

Secured credit cards can assist people with bad credit or don't have credit. It may sound odd however, not having a credit history could negatively affect the ability of a person to get credit. There is no guarantee that you will be accepted for a secured credit card, but the odds are greater.

Secured credit cards are one that you deposit funds into the account when it is first opened. This is considered to be a collateral deposit. If, for instance, $300 is made in the form of a payment to your card that is your credit line. This card will be "secured" through the value that was already given to the lender. Sometimes, additional funds can be added to increase the credit limit.

The money you deposit will be held by the bank and will not use to cover for the monthly bills. It is used as collateral and stored in an account for savings of some sort. The money will be returned to the client after the account has been closed. Don't believe you're going to find that your card provider is going to use the collateral deposit to pay for your monthly bills. If they do, that's not something you want to do! The aim is to begin making a record of paying your bill promptly, without relying on that collateral deposit.

Secured credit cards can be an excellent option for those who has poor credit or poor credit as they can help building your credit score, and they are able to look as regular credit cards to your credit score.

Secured cards also come with disadvantages. Certain cards might require an insurance policy, or other type of service when they offer the card. I have stayed clear of these offer.

Certain secured cards come with higher interest rates and an annual feethat is charged to your credit card each year. The annual fee could be as low as $25 and up to more than $85. It's a per-year cost to use their services.

Certain secured cards are accompanied by fees for application. There is a possibility of finding one that does not charge an application fee. If you choose this route, you must be sure to conduct your own research thoroughly and be sure to read the fine print prior to submitting your application. It is important to understand the specifics of your commitment before you start the account.

Before you apply before submitting an application, it's recommended to determine if the bank is reported to one of the major bureaus for credit. If not, you can skip the bank and go to that one. The bank should submit a credit report to the credit bureaus. That's the purpose of the card.

Ask your bank to mark your credit card as a secured one in your credit file. If they do not, do not apply for the card. The presence of a secured credit card by your credit score could damage your credit score. You would like the secured card to be seen on your credit report like normal credit card.

Important Note: Use the card only to make small purchases and make sure you pay the charge in full by the end of each month. The idea of carrying a account balance on a secured credit card is not a wise idea due to the excessive interest rates. It is also important to prove to the bank that you're committed to paying the account off monthly in full. This will increase the chances that you will be approved for an unsecure card at some point in the near future. Make sure you pay the bill in time. Create an automatic payment system for the bill, or some sort of automated reminder for yourself. Don't pay late on these payments.

It could take an entire year to build an impressive credit history using secured credit cards. Take your time and make sure you use the card in a responsible manner.

If you are a member of the credit union, you can inquire whether they can provide secured credit cards. They typically have lower rates of interest and may even waive the annual fee normally associated with secured credit cards.

Chapter 17: Eliminate Debt

The term "well-being" does not only refer to mental, physical and emotional well-being. Financial wellness is an integral part of our wellbeing as well. However, many of us ignore, or even deliberately disregard our financial health in relation to the subject of debt.

There are also times that we need to take a moment to examine our financial situation, not just the amount we make or spend. It's easy to ignore any debt we've accrued until we try to get loans, lease a home or find an employment. Then, our credit scores show what amount of credit we really have.

A good indicator for financial wellbeing is the ratio of debt to income. Experts suggest that people is obligated to pay 20percent of take-home income. For instance, a person who earns $1000 per month must reduce his debt to less than $200 per month. If his monthly car payment is at that level then he should not contemplate acquiring any additional obligations.

It's not an ideal scenario, but the reality is that a majority of us owe more than 20 percent of our income. It is not uncommon to be buried to the point of exhaustion with the midst of debt and feel overwhelmed by what to do to get rid of it.

Common causes of debt problems

Problems with debt, also known as "credit problems with credit" may be the result of many different behavior. The most frequently cited reasons are as follows:

1. In excess of the limits of one's financial resources

2. Unsuspecting spending, or incurring unnecessary costs

3. Poor budgeting can be caused by the inability to make an appropriate budget or failing to follow the budget that is already in place

4. Poor investments

5. Unforeseen situations, such as unexpected events, job losses health concerns, emergencies, and even death

How can you tell whether you're dealing with a debt issue? If you've ever been in one of these scenarios, you could be suffering from credit or debt problems.

There are times when you're late with your payments or scrambling to meet your due dates.

* You draw from your savings account to pay off bills and even essential needs such as food.

The majority of your monthly earnings go to pay off bills.

* You're no longer in a position to add funds to your savings.

* You don't have any savings, no matter what.

* You make use of credit cards or borrow money from people else to pay for the regular things that you pay with cash, like medications, groceries or even meals.

* You using cash advances on your credit card to pay other charges.

* You are able to make only the minimum amount of payments with any credit or debit cards.

* You've used up more than the limit of one credit card.

The balance on your credit card are increasing each month due to constant purchases, even if you are paying your bills on time.

* You do not know the amount you are owed.

You are always fighting with your family members over money.

* You should avoid receiving phone calls from collectors and creditors.

* You're several months late on your bill payment.

• Your account at the bank has been overdrawn or you've bounced a cheque or two.

* You've been refused credit.

There may be an additional incident that wasn't mentioned However, all of them are grave and require remediation.

If you were to lose your job tomorrow , would it be possible to make by paying for your daily necessities and paying off your debts until you can find a new job?

If your family member suddenly got sick and you were forced to pay all medical bills could you manage to live financially?

If you're more than certain that you'd experience a financial trouble if any of these scenarios occurred and it's safe to conclude that you've got an issue with debt. It's time to act to avoid it turning into a major catastrophe.

Pay back debts and raise your Credit Score

Your financial plan is an essential part of your debt repayment plan. Additionally there are a variety of things you must do when you plan to repay your debts.

• Follow repayment plans.

There are specific repayment plans for loans which you must adhere to. If you don't, you'll may end up paying more due to penalties, late fees and other costs.

Credit card loans come with due dates for payment that are specified on the invoices. Based on the issuer of your credit card there's typically a grace period to pay before the due date so that the purchase does not incur the cost of finance. You don't want to be liable for excessive interest charges and late fees rates because you didn't pay in time.

* Prioritize debts to be paid.

While you may want to settle all your debts in one go however your financial situation might not permit it. So, you'll have to decide which debts need priority to pay first. To accomplish this it is necessary to make an inventory of all debts with all the pertinent details included including the interest rate, repayment period, balances and the minimum monthly payment in the event of any.

Here are a few options you can consider:

Prioritize debts based on basic interest rates.

This strategy will allow you to be able to pay off debts with the highest rates of interest first. It is possible to speak with your lender or bank to see whether you are able to have the interest rate reduced prior to. This can lower the minimum amount you pay each month, allowing you to pay for them quicker, and also help you save money, too.

A lot of credit companies will reduce interest rates in order to keep customers. It's never hurt to ask.

O Prioritize debts based on the current rates of interest.

In contrast to simple interest, effective rate of interest takes into account the tax effects. This is evident more frequently in mortgages, student loans and similar types of loans.

Prioritize debts based on other charges.

There are loans or debts that charge additional fees aside from interest. If the fees are large and significant, they may affect the decision of which debt to settle first. There are many options to deal with these.

Beware of from "minimum payments syndrome".

Credit card bills provide you with an amount that is a minimum to keep your account up to date. Many cardholders just pay the minimum amount, not realizing that the minimum amount is only used to pay interest. A little extra can reduce the principal balance faster.

* Use to apply the "Snowball" as well as the "Snowflaking" approach.

It's a method of repayment for credit card debts (and it's the only situation that making the minimum monthly amount is actually advised). If you own multiple credit cards, classify them according to their respective interest rates.

As the amount you can on your first debt, the one that has the highest interest rate. Make sure you pay the minimum monthly installments on other credit cards.

After the first debt has been paid off, you can move on to the one that has the second highest rate of interest making as much payment as you can, and making in only minimum monthly payment on the other debts.

* Talk to lenders about loan terms.

There's nothing wrong with speaking to your creditors. Debtors are advised to be truthful with their lenders. The relationships that involve borrowing or lending money demand some level of trust. That's why it is essential to communicate clearly with lenders.

The process of negotiating with lenders could yield more favorable conditions. You can also negotiate with them to lower the interest rate. This can reduce the minimum amount you pay and allow you to pay off the principal. It is also possible to ask them to extend the loan term or time frame, which will give you more time to pay the loan.

How to avoid the negative impact of interest

You may be thinking about why prioritization of debt payments places a significant amount of emphasis on interest, which is the amount (which typically is a certain percent of the principal) to be paid by the creditor to the debtor in addition to the principal. It is the amount that the lender charges the borrower to make borrowing of money.

The basic idea behind interest is that it needs more money to lend money.

In most cases, interest is usually calculated as a monthly payments, which is the case with car loans as well as home loan. The interest charged on credit card accounts is included into the minimum amount to be paid.

The interest rates can are a negative influence on debt once they start to rise. As you repay debt, interest rates can pose bigger problems.

For instance, in the case of credit card debt. Like we said earlier the larger portion of the minimum payments cover interest, which is more than the initial debt. When you attempt to settle a debt with high interest rates you'll also pay more towards the finance charge , instead of the principal. This means that it will take longer to pay off that debt.

The only way to prevent this from happening is to make over the amount of minimum monthly payments stipulated. Make your monthly payments higher so that you can make more payments on the principal, which serves as the basis for calculating the interest. Naturally when the amount of loan outstanding decreases as does the amount of interest you'll be paying will decrease as well regardless of whether the interest rate remains the same.

Beware of Getting More Debt

After you've been able to get your debt out of the way You'll probably feel as if a burden is lifted off your shoulders. But it doesn't stop there.

At this point it is best to take an "been there been there, done that and never to repeat it" approach. You've already had the experience of being a burdened by obligations, and have tried everything to get rid of these debts. After you've made it you must ensure that it doesn't happen ever again.

Here are some simple suggestions to help you maintain complete control over your debts or, more simply, be debt-free.

1. Be careful with credit cards.

"Retail therapy" is a popular method used by people who are down and wish to get themselves up. The act of shopping produces dopamine in their bodies that can make them feel happier. Another reason for this is dependence.

If you're a habitual buyer and you're a frequent spending person, you should use money instead of credit. If you absolutely need to utilize a credit card make sure to pay the balance off during the grace period prior to when interest is added to the amount, which usually occurs 28 days following the purchase (check with the bank or credit card provider).

Only shop when you really require something. Be wary of being enticed by brochures, ads and catalogs. If you're one of those who buy things but never actually utilize the items, not only do the cost be reduced, but but you'll also reduce the space inside your home.

2. Reserve some funds to cover any emergencies.

Experts advise that everyone has at least six months' worth of living expenses saved. If you lose your job it is essential to know what you'd do to keep an enclosing on your head and food on the table, and clothing on your as well as your loved ones' backs.

A savings account for emergencies can to avoid having to rely on credit cards if the job you have lost, or your vehicle breaks down, or you are faced with an enormous medical bill.

3. Do not apply for loans

After you have paid off an outstanding debt, the final thing you'll want to do is to enter into another. If you have to purchase something so expensive that you have to borrow money then you must consider whether it's something that you actually require. It is recommended to consult your financial plans and determine if the loan is worth sabotaging your financial development.

4. Find alternative sources of income.

In addition, bringing in additional cash can help reduce debt by a large amount. If you're able to spare the time or want to increase your income, part-time jobs garage sales and side business are some options to explore. We'll look at possible sources of income the next chapter.

5. Create a financial document file.

Receipts, billsand statement from your bank... everything that is related to your finances, keep the information accordingly. Keep a record of the ledger or file folder of your debts. You can make sure to update them with any payments or other transactions that impact them, along with the date that you completed the transaction.

It's not only good recording, but it's also a means to be protected in the event that your creditors come after you over a payment that you've made. You'll have evidence to prove your dispute (e.g. receipts, bills). You can develop your own system for keeping records to keep track of these.

6. Get help.

There's no reason not to seek help from a professional in order to help you manage your credit and financial affairs.

A credit counselor's assistance is a good solution for your specific circumstance. There are many experts who offer credit counseling to people who are in serious financial difficulty. They analyze your financial circumstances and provide a reasonable solution.

Another benefit of working with credit counselor is the ability they provide to make a plan for managing debt. They can help you reduce the burden of debt and you'll be free sooner than you anticipated.

Obtain Credit Reports

Credit scores are the method the majority of lenders determine the degree to which they are willing to take the risk of lending you money. It's a measurement of your debt-to-income ratio as well as how creditors evaluate your credit history against lenders. A lot people don't have a clear picture of their credit scores, and then are shocked to discover that they're not quite so high as we expected.

In order to improve the credit rating of yours, you need to identify the amount and who you are owed. The most effective way to know this and monitor your debt is to get your credit reports from all from the three agencies. Each year, customers get a free credit account from any of the three businesses: TransUnion, Equifax and Experian.

Creditors are required to report to one of these organizations. They keep track of the amount you owe each creditor have owed, whether your account is in good standing, and the number of days in arrears you are. This is a fantastic way to know exactly the amount you owe, if you are unable to remember all the accounts and loans you've opened.

When you keep track of your reports, you will be able to spot any errors that could lower the credit rating. If you spot any inaccurate or incorrect information, you may dispute it and have the information removed from your report. 25% of people discover inaccurate information in their reports.

Another method of monitoring the score of your credit report is to sign up for an online credit monitoring service. Credit Karma can be a no-cost service that will provide your TransUnion as well as Equifax scores and informs you of any changes that is added to your credit report.

The first step is to pay off your debts. This is the best step to increase your score on credit. Another option is to create a positive payment history. When you begin to pay the debts you owe, it is important to establish an account of your payments that every creditor will report in the credit bureaus. The more successful your repayment record and the better your credit score, the more it gets better. Because you're only able to receive each year's report You may want to schedule your requests. This will allow you to keep track of the same report every four months.

Example:

In January, you ask for your report through Experian. After that, you seek you report through Equifax at the end of May. Then, you request your reports through Transunion at the end of September. Your reports are kept in rotation to ensure you are aware of any new activity, and also dispute any negative information that is released.

Chapter 18: What to Fund For An Emergency Fund Effectively

Most financial crises arise due to not having enough savings, or having enough savings put aside in case an unexpected event occurs. A very crucial factors in repairing your credit is taking prudent steps to increase your credit score. You should also try to avoid a financial crisis from occurring ever again. It's a lot of work to return to your path and increase your score on credit. The most important thing you do not want is for catastrophe to strike again. One way to avoid this is to establish an emergency fund for your household.

The majority of experts suggest that an emergency fund include at least 3 to 6 months worth in living costs. Also, you should consider the possibility that if you quit your current job it could take up to six months to find a replacement one, especially if earned at a higher level or there are many others within your area of expertise. In the event of illness or unemployment, it can have an impact on your financial situation.

If you've not been saving consistently up to the present, it might be difficult to establish an habit of savings However, as we've mentioned, we're sure there are areas of your budget where you can be tightened. the short-term sacrifices you make in the coming few weeks and months could be the basis for longer-term security.

Your main goal will be to reduce credit card debt in order to boost your credit score, as the rates of interest you're paying on the balances of your credit cards are significantly higher than those that you would earn from a savings or money market account or money market account or any other investment that is liquid which is an investment where you have access to the cash should you ever require to.

With that said, make sure you leave some extra cash in case to ensure that you're not in a rush to use your credit cards and have open accounts in your bank for any anticipated expenses that you anticipate. For instance, a holiday club is a popular way to spread the costs of Christmas including food, gifts, entertainment, as well as travel over a number of months. Thanks to modern technology, you will receive an email reminder telling you when your next payment is due to be made, or the money can be taken from your account on a regular basis.

Other things to consider are trips to visit family members or other unusual day care expenses during summer, when your children aren't in school, particularly in the case that both of you work and don't have many days off.

Jim has written a complete guide to creating an emergency fund. The guide includes steps-by-step instructions. In the meantime, it's enough to suggest you must save each month a portion of your savings to protect yourself against unexpected expenses.

It's not sensible to place a large amount of money into an account for savings in this moment However, especially if you're paying high interest on the balances of your credit cards. It is possible to put a small amount of money aside each month however, you should make the remainder of your funds be used for your benefit by paying off your credit card debt.

If you're 50 to 75 percent your way to paying off your credit card debts and you've been making snowballs of your payment from old cards, you should start directing some of the funds you've been putting into pay down your debts in the quickest time possible.

It is then logical to start building an emergency fund. After all credit cards have been paid in full it is then possible to build up your emergency fund by accumulating 6 months worth of expenses, based on your budget. Do not go overboard and start thinking that you are able to take a break financially. Keep working towards being debt free and staying out of debt, and establishing the most secure financial future.

Save money in your emergency fund, as well as other savings accounts to fund things that are essential for you as well as your loved ones. Be aware that you aren't required to make use of credit cards again, unless there's an underlying reason to do this, like cash back or funds in 529 accounts. You should restrict your spending in order to stay in line with your good ways of life and to not spend every penny you earn.

One of the most effective method to accomplish this is to never ignore any bill. Examine your bills for utilities as well as your cable bills, mobile phones and many more to discover the most cost-effective bargains. Your money is yours. So, make every cent count and let the savings be used for your benefit by paying off the amount of debt you have and improving the credit rating. After you've accomplished this, you'll be able to begin to think more than just about saving money, but also investing in the right way as well.

Another thing to examine in relation to emergency situations is whether you are covered enough, and what is the appropriate type of insurance. Jim discusses the topic of life insurance within his beginners guide to this topic, and there's several different insurance options that can assist in coping with unexpected situations. Insurance can protect you in the event of an emergency and help keep costs under control. Insurance for pets is vital these days, with the average emergency pet treatment at the vet costing more than $3000.

As we've said, making a budget, saving, and managing your budget by reviewing your financials frequently and paying off your debt in a strategic manner will aid in improving your score on credit. Making sure you are protecting what you have and saving for the unexpected and being prepared before an emergency occurs again can protect you from the types of financial catastrophes that could have caused you to be in financial trouble at all in the first place.

When we talk about budgets with our clients We always remind them that they're supposed to allow for flexibility to permit some flexibility, but not a rigid one, however, they should not be too flexible that you end up experiencing financial problems over and over repeatedly. One area that most people do not consider when they budget is the line that relate with their earnings.

Steps to Take

1-Open a brand new bank account for savings at a financial institution or credit union. You should look for one that offers interest or no charges. You can use this account as an emergency fund and never use it unless there's the possibility of a financial emergency.

2. Open additional accounts if they aren't subject to fees, to save money for additional financial objectives. Set up a 529 account when it is available in your state and you'd like to fund colleges for your children that you have. Create a Christmas club account in case you have lots of Christmas commitments to the

holidays you would like to budget for over the entire twelve months of the year , rather than only one.

3. Make a list of your savings goals beginning with short-term goals and then long-term and mid-term goals.If you want to, you can put an amount of money on each goal. Make a note of the date you'd like to achieve the goal, for example, the day your first child is due to go to college. Review the balances of the accounts you created in Step 2 frequently to determine whether you're in line with your goals.

In this guide, we've been talking about getting out of financial difficulties using the current amount of income, based on the way things are as they are at present, and assuming that there is no change other than attempting to save money so that you can pay down the debts faster.

But what if you make a small modification or two your spouse and you, or perhaps your children doing some work to increase the income in your family? Doing a second job, or creating your own small company can help generate more income to pay off your financial obligations and help improve your credit score more quickly. Let's take a look at this issue within the following chapter.

Chapter 19: What's my Credit Limit?

In terms of what your limit on credit is, perhaps the first thing to understand is what your actual limit is. Before you decide whether you'd like to increase it then you need to know your current limit. There are two simple methods to verify:

The information should appear on your statement. When I look at my statement for credit cards (either on paper or on the internet) I get an overview of my account. This usually contains the balance total as well as the total amount due as well as the total amount I have to pay and also the amount of credit I have available. The same should be true for all credit cards.

You can contact them by phone - There is an 800 number printed on the back of the card. If you make an email, they will be able to inform you of the limit.

As you will see, it's quite simple! If you're not sure the limit of your credit try one of these actions and discover!

WHAT CREDIT LIMITS DO YOU HAVE? INCREASES AFFECTS credit score

When discussing the possibility of a credit limit increase many are worried that it could result in an adverse effect to their score. Are they right to be concerned? Absolutely and not.

A request for an increase to your credit limit could negative impact your credit score over the short-term. Since it could trigger an inquiry into your credit score which can cause your score to drop. This is why I would not suggest soliciting an increase anytime close to the time you'll be applying for the mortgage, car loan or any other loan where the interest rate is contingent on the credit scores of your.

But in the long term, the greater credit utilization resulting from an increased amount of credit can more than compensate for the dip in short-term. The credit score of thirty percent can be calculated by amount you owe as well as the proportion of the amount you owe in relation to your credit limits. If you don't spend as much as the increase (a significant point) The larger limit will decrease the credit utilization ratio which will improve your score.

In the end... the request for an increase in your credit limit may be detrimental in the near term, but will can help you in the long run. In the same way we've discussed how it will improve your credit utilization , which can have a positive effect on your credit score.

STRENGHTEN your case for a CREDIT LIMIT Increase

If you're asking for an increase in the credit limits of your account, then most likely possible scenario is that you'll be refused. This could result in a drop on your score (from inquiries about credit) but not give you the full benefits of a higher limit.

You're likely to need to do as efficient of an effort as you can in ensuring that the creditor is willing to grant your request, and even increase the limit. How do you achieve that? Here are some suggestions to assist:

- Ensure that your payments are made on time. If you've made any payments late then it's probably not the best time to inquire to increase your limit. You must maintain a track record that you pay your bill on time and timely manner so that your creditor can be assured that you're trustworthy with a larger limit.

Pay the balance on your credit card. If you're nearing the limit of your card, asking for a higher limit can make it appear like you're in a state of desperation, and businesses aren't willing to give more cash at someone who is desperate, as this could pose risk for them. Make sure you pay the bill in the amount you can and then ask for an increase.

- Pay off any additional debts, if you can. You'll need to do all you can to demonstrate to your creditor that you'll be able to repay the credit card regardless of the amount. As little other debt as is possible and this will help them feel more at ease.

Time is your friend. If you've just opened a bank account, 2 months later isn't the ideal time to make an inquiry. You should wait until you've had it for a while, and you have built up trust and time with the business. This will give you greater chance of the success.

If you've taken the initiative to increase your limit, the worst thing you'd like to see happen is to see your request rejected as it means that you won't be able to request it again for a long time. Take your time before you submit your request and ensure that your argument is as convincing as it could be.

Chapter 20: What Does It All Mean?

Credit scores can vary between 300 at 850 or more points. Your position on this range can differ from month to the next , based on the information on your report. Like your health, it's your responsibility to ensure that you maintain your credit. If you notice something is not right and you want to fix it, you need to take the necessary steps to correct it. To do this you need to be able to manage your credit effectively. In order to accomplish this, you must understand how credit machines work.

You can search for credit repair companies, and you'll find a lot of them on the scene ready to accept your money and help you to get back on the right track. Unfortunately, the majority of these are scams , and the ones who are legitimate offer only the basics of what to do. Most of the time the things listed are ones you can accomplish on your own without assistance from outside. Their primary goal is to show you how to fix problems. They don't aid you in understanding how credit actually operates and how you can prevent yourself from getting into the negative credit trap once more.

Understanding Your FICO Score

Nearly every creditor would like to check an FICO score before deciding to offer you credit. Knowing what these numbers represent can make a big difference in determining and taking control of your financial situation. When you learn more about the way that the system operates it will help you to be more confident. While other aspects will be considered on the outcome, anyone seeking to boost their creditworthiness has to begin at the FICO score, as the majority of financial decisions are based upon it.

One of the most important things you need to know is your scoring range, so you will know what the meaning of your number is.

800+ is a high score that is thought to be a lot higher than the average. Anybody who scores this high can expect to obtain credit approval for almost everything they need. Unfortunately, only one percent of people fall into this group.

740-799 is thought to be excellent. Although it's not among the most impressive but it's still considered as being above the average. Anyone who falls in this group will be eligible for higher rates of interest and a broad variety of credit options.

670-739 is thought to be acceptable and is around average. They're not the ideal buyer, but they are thought to be within what is known as the "acceptable" spectrum.

580-669 is considered an acceptable score. They are typically lower than average and are referred to as subprime lenders. This means that even though they are able to get credit, it is very difficult for them. Their interest rate will likely be more, and they are often required to make larger payments on the transactions they purchase.

579-669 is considered to be a low score. The people who fall within this category are usually dismissed outright by many areas of business. But, they are able to obtain credit under different types. For instance, they could have the ability to get credit cards that are secured, or they might require an amount of money to secure the approval they require.

This is only a basic outline of the way in which it is that the FICO scores are broken into pieces. Consideration of your payment history as well as your debt amount you have and the kind of credit you've got can help identify what your score is.

It is crucial to keep in mind the fact that credit scores will not stay the same throughout your entire life. Each month your creditors send information about your transactions to credit bureaus. Therefore, your score will always require adjustment. There are also other elements to consider that Fair Isaac Corporation also factors into your score that might not be as apparent. For instance, your income or the time you've worked working is not a significant factor in your credit score. Additionally, those with no credit history or have a short history of credit will generally score lower than those who have more credit history to be able to report. A lower credit score doesn't necessarily stem from late payments, or perhaps being in debt above your head. Sometimes, it's caused by something completely beyond your control.

In the section of your account history which is probably one of the most thorough sections of the report You will get the majority of the information regarding the account you. It'll look like this:

Name of the creditor: This can refer to the creditor or merchant who issued the information.

Number of your account: It could be the unique number for your account. In most instances, the information you provide will be encrypted to guard your privacy and prevent anyone from accessing your account details.

Type of Account This section will determine the type of account, whether it's a loan, automobile loan or mortgage or revolving credit card (like credit cards).

Responsibility: Indicates if you are the sole user with access to the account or whether others are allowed to use the account.

Payment Record: Defines what the minimum payment requirement is for the account.

Date of opening The exact date on which the account was created.

Data reported on: latest date on which the creditor supplied details at the credit bureau.

Balance: the amount due in the current account.

Credit limit What is the maximum credit limit you are able to use.

Credit score that is high or high balance The largest amount of credit you've been able to use on your account.

Past Due The total amount of debt overdue.

Status of payment: Is the account current, overdue or is it an account that is a charge-off (meaning it's not made a payment for a long time, and the company doesn't think you'll make a payment).

Payment history: Shows how often you've made payments since the account established.

Collector accounts could be any account that were transferred to a collection company.

Credit Inquiries

The report also keeps an inventory of how many instances there was an inquiry regarding your credit. Inquiries that are a lot of times with no credit being issued can have a negative impact on your credit score. It's a sign you've tried to secure credit but been rejected numerous times, this could cause a lender to consider a second thought before deciding to offer credit to your application.

There are two types of credit inquiries that you need to be aware of. The first is a "soft" inquiry and is that are made by lenders who want reasons to promote their products. Maybe credit card companies are seeking new customers. The other, "hard" inquiries are the ones that you've already applied to. Maybe a bank that offers credit cards or a department store or even a gas company.

Public Records

Public records is the place where you'll discover information on anything legally relevant with your credit. If you've been through a bankruptcy, court judgements and tax liens or any other information should be recorded on this page. However, this list isn't for all things that are related to your legal affairs, but only for things that are related directly to credit. If you've had a criminal record or convictions, they are not part of your credit report, unless they have an impact on your credit (passing fraudulent checks to make payments the balance on your credit card, as an instance).

In the ideal scenario, you should ensure that this section in your file is and completely clear. Any mistakes in this area could be a significant factor in your score , and may hinder you from obtaining any kind of credit.

The positive side is that when you've got a poor report, the bad records are not able to remain on your report for a long time. The majority of information will be in your file for 7 to 10 years. Questions will stay on your report for the maximum period of two years. This means that over time, the negative aspects will fade and, as long as you keep an acceptable standing your credit score will increase naturally.

It is true that the Fair Isaacs Corporation is very secretive about the exact method they use to determine the scores, but at least you'll are aware of what they're looking for and what areas of your report must be enhanced to boost your overall score.

How to Read Your Report

When you first get the report, it will likely be difficult to understand. Once you understand the contents of each section however, it's much easier to figure out what it tells you about yourself. But, you'll likely prefer to pay closer attention to the next section, which is the full account of your past financial background.

To begin, you should look for mistakes or errors that could be reported. You'll be shocked at how many mistakes are found in credit reports. For instance, insurance companies that claim that the deductible didn't get payed, or the payments were late, even though they were not. Make sure you find the mistakes and mark them. This will be the first issues you'll address when looking to increase your score.

Once you've got the mistakes noted, search for anything that could be fake. Credit cards you don't actually possess, such as. They could be an indication that your identity is compromised and could be a cause for issues that be a problem, you'll want to address them promptly.

If you've got all the negatives of your credit uncovered It is now time to formulate an action plan that can help improve your credit score.

Since the society which has been shaped by technological advances, but not necessarily reasoning with humans, mistakes happen often. Incorrect information on your credit report can have serious consequences and should be addressed promptly. It is obvious that the faster you find out these errors more quickly you will be able to take the necessary steps to repair your reputation and improve your credit score.

Your Credit Utilization Ratio

Then, you should take a look at the credit utilization ratio, which is the ratio of your credit card balance in relation to the credit limit you have. It is essential to know that this ratio will comprise an important portion in your FICO score, and is the second most important to your payments history.

A high ratio suggests that you could have a problem with your spending and are becoming over the top in debt. When lenders see this, they'll immediately begin to believe that you're in danger of defaulting on your payment.

If you have a high rate of credit utilization could be crucial in the process of establishing an excellent credit score. It will help make up for some of the negative points of your credit, at least until you begin taking steps to remove these.

In general, the less your ratio is, the more attractive your see on the paper. A ratio of 0% indicates that you have not used all your credit available. Credit ratios of 30% or less percent or less is the minimum that creditors are seeking. Anything more than that will result in your credit score to decrease.

How to Reduce Your Credit Utilization Ratio

Likely as you would expect, your credit utilization ratio fluctuates constantly. Each payment you make your ratio drops and each time you make use of your creditaccount, the ratio goes up.

The most effective method to improve your score is to reduce the credit card credit card. This is the fastest method of bringing your percentage down. Spend the maximum amount you can to the total balance, and don't buy any more items until you're less than 30%.

Another option to reduce your ratio is to request your creditor to increase the limit. It may be difficult for those who already have credit issues, but the greater you can spend on credit, the less your ratio. That is if you cease using your credit card until you are lower than that threshold of 30.

Being able to understand the details of the credit reports is among the most crucial ways to boost the credit rating. Once you've figured out what you should be looking for and know exactly the areas that need fixing It is crucial to start figuring out an action plan to increase your credit score and put you in a better position with prospective lenders. In the coming two chapters, we'll examine a number of ways that you can do to help you put an optimistic spin on your credit score.

Chapter 21: Improve Your Credit Score in 30 Days

As you've already discovered from the text, a greater credit score can mean lower interest rates on mortgages as well as better credit card deals and higher rates for insurance. Also, you should know that you don't have to wait for a long time to increase your credit score. A 30-day period of time is sufficient to dramatically increase your score and get your sights on getting a high score (750or higher). All you have to know is what you need to do.

Step 1: Carry Out A Comprehensive Diagnosis

The first step to do is to determine the root of your lower-than-perfect score. The easiest method to do this is to take a look at the questions below and keep an eye on the "yes" answers you provide.

1. Do you make late payments on your credit cards?

The primary factor that affects your credit score is your credit past. Paying late can impact your credit score rapidly (and significantly negatively as well). Each month, your installment payment helps to build your credit score slowly however what it will take to destroy everything, and shift a number of points back, is a single unpaid payment. Any gains you've achieved will be quickly reversed. If you fail to pay a bill on or before the due date, just make sure that you pay in the quickest time possible due to lending institutions' an inclination to wait for 30 days to expire (from the date of payment) before reporting the payment.

2. Have your cards been are at their maximum?

Your credit utilization ratio adds in your score in the same extent as your credit history. When we talk about the term "credit utilization," we refer to the total credit card debt compared to the credit limit. For example, if all credit cards are fully loaded, it indicates the credit usage is high. In certain circles, this is known as "amounts due". For example, if you have a balance of $3,000 and a credit of $4,000 the utilization rate is 75% which is a poor ratio. It is recommended to maintain the ratio at a decent 25% or lower.

3. Do you close your old accounts, or maybe only account that you consider recent?

The age average of your credit account is a significant factor. As time passes, you'll receive points from this category. This is the reason why you shouldn't close accounts that are old. Don't close accounts you've already paid off.

4: Do only make use of one type of credit?

Credit bureaus want to know that you're capable to manage a variety different credit offerings. For example, mortgages, auto loans, and student loan are each installment that is why they are all grouped into one category of credit. The reason for this is that the amount is fixed. But the home equity line or credit card is eligible for the category of revolving credit. Credit bureaus will see you in a favorable image if you've got both apart from having only one kind of credit.

5: Do your look for new types of credit?

Each inquiry made into your credit or credit application could affect your credit score by many points.

Soft inquiries, such as those that help you qualify for various promotions Self-checks, self-checks, and employer checks won't negatively impact your credit score. However, hard inquiries (those that are the consequence of applying for credit) however, can certainly affect your score. They are the ones that will be avoided.

Second Step: Retification and Strategies To Improve Your Credit Score

For each "yes" answer you answered, there is at the very least one credit-related aspect that could be contributing to your low credit score. The suggestions below can aid you in devising a personalised plan to boost your credit score.

1. Check your free credit report for the year to ensure there are no errors.

The Fair Credit Reporting Act, FCRA is a law that requires each of the three national credit reporting firms: Experian, TransUnion and Equifax will offer you a complimentary credit report on your request, each 12 months. It is the Federal Trade Commission, FTC is the US agency for protecting consumers is responsible for applying the FCRA in relation to the companies that report on credit. All you have to do is to order your free copy from annualcreditreport.com (please note that this is the only authorized website for getting free credit reports- it amalgamates credit scores from the 3 credit reporting companies). You can also call them at 1-877-322-8228. They will ask you to supply names, SSN, date of birth, as well as your address to verify your identity. Another method by which you can receive your free credit report is by completing an Annual Credit Report Request Form to be sent to:

Keep in mind that you won't need to request a report from each credit reporting agency individually, as they all work together to provide free reports through annualcreditreport.com. Keep in mind that you are able to request reports from all companies at a time, one at a or all at once. Learn more about how to get your free annual credit report by visiting the FTC website.

Here's something you have to understand:

It is crucial to review all three credit reports:

A common mistake that people make is to only look at the credit report of one business and don't look at the others. They believe that they'll simply read the same information regardless, and therefore they don't need to look them up. If you're in this type of situation it is essential to recognize that there likely to be minor distinctions in all three credit reports. There's always the possibility that you'll be missing something by not examining all the others. In some instances the information you do not know can be the difference in an excellent credit score and low one, as well as causing you to miss out on the credit line you're trying to get. Your credit score could be affected by the different reporting that is present on all three reports. For example, if one of the three bureaus doesn't have information regarding your old account and it's FICO credit score calculated from this report is likely to be lower than the two other. So, make sure that you go through all 3 credit reports thoroughly. So, you'll not miss anything and will be able to create the most effective method to improve your credit score by utilizing your knowledge base.

Some experts suggest it is better to ask for credit reports at various times throughout the year, to be able to effectively keep track of your advancement. If you think it's best to obtain all of your credit reports at one at the same time, it is possible to request statements at any time of the year in order to monitor your improvement. It will certainly cost the cost of.

2. How do you find statements within the mini-periods?

NOTE: No other service provides a free credit report other than annualcreditreport.com. Any other business that claims to provide a free report will at some moment, later require a deposit. If any free credit-monitoring service requests your credit card information It could be fraudulent!

The best method to obtain credit reports during the mini period, which is also outside of the annual report that is required it is to go by using services that offer the identical. You'll definitely have to The most beneficial free services available to your needs right now are:

Credit Karma

Nerd Wallet

Credit Sesame

WalletHub

Mint.com

AAA Membership

The top paid services are:

LifeLock

TrustedID

IdentityGuard

Privacy Guard

MyFico

Be aware of such mistakes for example:

Late payments reported in reports that are older seven years older

Accounts that may not be yours

You have paid off, but show as unpaid

Accounts dismissed in bankruptcy, and are showing as indelinquent or have an outstanding balance

Tax liens are cleared and paid, and are at least seven years old

Also, you should be looking out for:

Names and addresses that are incorrect

Inaccurate employer information

Although these personal mistakes may not impact your credit score but they could be an indication of fraud, reporting errors or another type of bad playing.

If you find such mistakes The next step to take is to file a dispute against these with your credit reporting bureau. The next chapter after this one will provide guidance on this. But, remember that it you are entitled to get these errors corrected within the period of 30 days (45 days is the maximum in the event that the credit bureau requires additional time to look over any documentation you may have included.)

2. Improve your credit utilization in order to boost your credit score an immediate boost

There are two ways you could go about this. If you're able to apply them quickly and quickly, your credit score can be raised in just 30 days. The two methods are:

Make a massive payment to pay off the credit card credit card

The fact is that the credit rating of yours will naturally increase as your credit card balances decrease. Particularly, if pay off the credit card over the limit, you could effectively give your credit score an increase of up to 100 points in just 30 days. In reality the dollar value do not really matter. What is important is the debt amount you carry expressed in terms of a percentage of the credit amount you're allowed.

You can increase your credit limit, without having to increased amount of debt

For example, if you have a credit card balance of $1500, and an amount of credit that is $3,000, the ratio will be at 50 percent. This isn't ideal. But, if the lender raises the credit limit to about $6000, this will allow you to reduce the credit utilization rate to 25 percent. This is pretty impressive and you've done this without paying any money to reduce your balance. If you're planning to try this method, ensure you have a good credit score.

3. If you have bad credit, try different types of credit cards

This will boost your score fast.

There is a chance that you have had a few poor financial choices or experienced poor management skills in the past, and your credit score is suffering because of it. There is a chance that you will have difficulties obtaining an ordinary credit card which you can use later to improve your credit.

If this is the case you might want to consider an unsecured credit card to get you started on your way to building a solid track history of repaying the debt on time.

Secured credit cards requires the deposit of a security security that is refundable, that you are required to pay. The card's issuer utilizes this amount as collateral or security. What you're doing is protecting your credit limit on your secured credit card by using the amount you deposit. Once you have done this you can combine the responsible actions in the future together with the other strategies discussed in this section.

The next step is to discuss how you can deal to correct any mistakes could be found on you credit file.

Conclusion

The principal goal in this publication was to assist you build your credit score to ensure that you're more financially secure. You'll be able to get loans quickly during times of crises and will not need to travel from one place to another to obtain approval. Additionally, you will be able enjoy your life , as many credit card businesses are willing to issue cards that you can use to do your shopping.

I hope you'll use the many concepts in this book and put them to great use. I also hope that you be careful not to make the mistakes described in chapter 4 because it is essential to follow the correct things and not doing things that aren't right to improve your score.

Try doing everything right while avoiding any mistakes, and if you still think you are not good and you need help, then consult an organization that will to help you improve your credit score. I wish you the best of luck in your endeavour and hope that you can repair your credit and turn it to a better one as quickly as you can!